Best Wishes

Paddi Clark

Sugar Flowers

for Beginners

Paddi Clark

First published in March 2008 by
B. Dutton Publishing Limited, Alfred
House, Hones Business Park, Farnham,
Surrey, GU9 8BB.

Copyright: Paddi Clark 2008

ISBN-13: 978-1-905113-08-8

*I dedicate this book to my
wonderful family – to my
husband and solemate, Bruce,
and my three sons, Oliver,
Lawrence and Toby, for all
their fantastic support, love,
encouragement, help and
continuous sense of humour,
accompanied with much
laughter, and especially for
putting up with the 'infernal
boxes'! My love, as always, and
enormous gratitude to you all,
for caring so very much. I am
truly fortunate to have you all
in my life.*

Publisher: Beverley Dutton
Editor: Jenny Stewart
Art Director/Designer: Sarah Richardson
Copy Editor: Clare Porter
Sub Editor: Jenny Royle
Design Assistant: Zena Manicom
Photography: Alister Thorpe
Printed in Slovenia

Foreword

I was absolutely delighted to have the opportunity to write the foreword for this book, written by a friend who shares my great passion for flowers and love of sugarcraft.

I have known Paddi for many years; I have always been a great admirer of her superbly innovative sugarcraft skills. I have a wonderful memory of a glorious cake which was topped by a globe – simply stunning. Her wall decoration of sugar poppies was absolutely wonderful and is a treasured memory.

Paddi and I have taught together on a number of occasions at the Squires Kitchen Summer Schools; the day of the London bombings really put Paddi to the test. Despite being incredibly anxious about her beloved husband, Bruce, who was in London for a meeting, Paddi managed to focus on her work and made the class as happy and informative as ever. It was a great test of her wonderful nature. Paddi's classes are both informative and fun, enabling students of all abilities to achieve results far beyond their expectations.

I am sure this book will be a wonderful addition to every sugarcrafter's library.

Tombi Peck

Founder Member, British Sugarcraft Guild

I met Paddi around twenty years ago and we have remained good friends through our shared passion for sugarcraft. We have worked together at many sugarcraft exhibitions and we both have the same desire to teach this wonderful craft to students of all ages and abilities.

I am so pleased that Paddi has put together a book on making sugar flowers for beginners. Showing a real flower alongside her step-by-step method for replicating it in sugar adds a new dimension to the craft, keeping the focus on working from the source. Her teaching experience gives the reader a feeling of being guided through each piece, breaking down all the parts then bringing them together to create a beautiful, delicate piece of art.

I am sure that beginners to sugar floristry will find this book an invaluable resource and have no doubt that *Sugar Flowers for Beginners* will soon become the ultimate guide to flower making.

Eddie Spence MBE

National and international sugarcraft judge and former president of the British Sugarcraft Guild

Acknowledgements

I am very grateful to Beverley and Robert Dutton for giving me the opportunity to write this book – so I say a big thank you to you both. I feel honoured and privileged to have been asked.

I would also like to say thank you to the talented publishing team – Clare Porter who deciphered and planned my text, Jenny Stewart for her professional editing skills, Sarah Richardson for her expert design and layout of the book, Alister Thorpe for the fine photography, and not forgetting everyone in the Squires Kitchen office and shop for creating a friendly atmosphere to be in.

A heart-warming thank you to my sisters, Jenny and Chrissie, for their continued encouragement.

I am hugely and immensely grateful for the support from my family, my husband Bruce and sons Oliver, Lawrence, and Toby, for always being there for me both in practical help and honest opinions, and for not minding too much with sugarcraft encroaching on our lives! You have all been of tremendous help, which I could not have done without.

Thank you to you all.

You can do anything if you have enthusiasm.

Enthusiasm is the yeast that makes your hope rise to the stars.

Enthusiasm is the spark in your eye, and the swing in your gait, the grip in your hand, the irresistible surge of your will and the energy to execute your ideas…

Enthusiasm is at the bottom of all progress.

Henry Ford

Introduction

Having had the good fortune to be involved with all aspects of sugarcraft and teaching for over two decades, I have had the pleasure and privilege to teach many talented people and see their skills evolve in the craft.

Nature has given us the beauty of flowers, which are truly amazing, and to be able to recreate them in some small way like the real thing is a true delight.

Ever since I started to learn the art of sugarcraft, flowers have always been a joy to make, with their many intricate elements, petals and leaves; the different parts assembled together to make a creation, which comes to life, whether on a cake or to brighten a room in a showcase. To assemble the flower on its own, with its accompanying leaves or, indeed, in a simple arrangement, can be truly satisfying, especially to the beginner whose comment is often, "I will never be able to do that". To see their excitement and pleasure at their achievement is extremely rewarding.

So it is for those people and all the newcomers to this wonderful craft – not forgetting those of us who have been sugarcrafting for several years and are still enjoying what we do – that I have written this book. I hope you will be able to achieve what you see on the pages with success, and that you can be inspired by some small tip or idea that sparks off a creative thought, either to use or pass on to others.

Welcome to my book – I hope you enjoy it.

*Love
Paddi*

Contents

A to Z of Flowers and Leaves

Projects

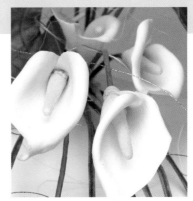

Basic Equipment, Materials and Techniques

To complete the projects in this book, you will require the materials and equipment listed here. Whilst some flowers call for specialist items such as particular cutters or veiners, this list covers the basic requirements for all the flowers in this book. I have described the techniques for their use, so if you are new to flower making this should help you get started. The tools are readily available from sugarcraft and cake decorating stockists and there are several manufacturers, so choose whichever works best for you. Make sure you always keep your equipment clean and use solely for sugarcraft projects.

Equipment

1 Non-stick rolling board

These are available in different sizes and colours (depending on the manufacturer) – I would recommend using a coloured board rather than a white one, as it is more restful on the eyes. Some boards have grooves within them to create ridges in the paste for wired petals and leaves; this type of board can also be turned over and used as a flat, non-stick surface.

2 Non-stick rolling pin

A small, non-stick, polypropylene rolling pin is an essential piece of equipment for rolling the paste smooth and thin. Rolling pins are available in different sizes but a medium size (around 23cm/9") is the most useful for flower making.

3 Ball/bone tool

These tools come in several different forms, depending on the manufacturer. A dog bone-shaped tool, whether in metal or plastic, is more useful than the straight variety. This tool is generally used with a foam pad (see no. 4).

4 Food-grade foam pad

This is a firm sponge pad which softens when pressure is applied to the surface. It is used in conjunction with a ball tool to thin and soften the edges of petals and leaves (details of this technique are described below), making them more realistic.

Technique: Frilling and softening

Place the leaf or petal onto the pad and roll the ball tool gently over the edge of the paste, half on the paste and half on the pad. This softens the edges of the paste, removes the cut edge and adds a gentle undulation or more of a defined curl to the leaf or petal, depending on the pressure used. It may take some practice to get the movement correct and achieve the desired effect.

5 Small palette knife

A small palette knife is an essential piece of equipment. They are available in different sizes, from very small to a medium size, either as a cranked or straight version, so use whichever you find most comfortable.

6 Dresden tool

Sometimes referred to as a veining tool, the thin end is used for veining the centre of leaves and petals, and the broad end is used to soften and flatten the edges and also flute them. The final result is different to the effect that is created using a ball tool.

7 CelStick

The CelStick has two differently-shaped ends: a pointed end for creating the centre of flowers and a rounded end, which can be used to open the paste wider if required. This tool can also be used as a small rolling pin. Available in small, medium and large, I find the medium size is the most useful.

8 Fine, pointed scissors

These are often used to cut the edges of calyces and petals from templates and to tidy up edges if required. The finer the point of the scissors (i.e. the narrower the tips), the easier they are to use.

9 Wires

Covered floristry wires are used to give petals and leaves extra support. They come in a variety of gauges (widths) – the higher the gauge number, the finer the wire (e.g. 30-gauge is a thinner wire than 24-gauge). The gauge you require will depend on the size of the petal or leaf you are making (i.e. large petals need more support and therefore thicker or lower-gauge wires). Wires are also available in a range of different colours but I tend to use white when wiring a petal or a pale leaf and green for the darker leaves so that the wire is not as visible in the finished piece. There are several methods for wiring petals and leaves – full instructions are given on pages 18 to 22.

10 Wire cutters and pliers

Wire cutters are needed for trimming floristry wires. A pair of fine-nosed pliers is essential for bending the wire into the desired shape and can also be useful for holding the wired ends whilst you work on the leaves and petals.

11 Craft knife

Use a craft knife to trim the paste where necessary and cut out freehand shapes. It is advisable not to do this when the paste is on the rolling board as you may damage the surface.

12 Leaf and petal veiners

One-piece and double-sided veiners are used to emboss sugar petals and leaves with a natural, veined pattern. I tend to use double-sided veiners as they create the most realistic finish, veining the front and back of the petal or leaf. A vast range of veiners is available for all different flower and leaf varieties and most brands can be purchased from sugarcraft shops.

13 Cutters/templates

Cutters make recreating a natural leaf or petal shape quick and easy – many different cutters are available from a number of specialist manufacturers. If you do not have the cutters you need, templates are a good alternative. These can be made quite accurately by pressing the real leaf or petal flat then tracing the outline onto a piece of paper before cutting the shape out. You can also draw the required shape freehand if you only have the picture of the real leaf or petal to hand. It is important to remember that some flowers and leaves are poisonous and must not come into direct contact with edible items.

14 Plain-edge cutting wheel

Cutting wheels have a large and a small wheel and can be used for a multitude of sugarcraft tasks. They are particularly useful in sugar floristry for cutting out leaves and petals from paste, either freehand or using a template as a guide.

15 Paintbrushes

It is advisable to have a good selection of good quality, man-made bristle brushes to hand when making sugar flowers as these produce the best effects when dusting colour onto petals and leaves. Different sized brushes are available; I frequently use nos. 5 to 10 flat brushes and nos. 00 to 4 round brushes. Both types of brush have their uses – flat brushes are more efficient for dusting large areas while round brushes will reach into smaller areas of the flower (e.g. the centre) and are better suited for painting on fine details, like spots and lines.

16 Tweezers

It is worth investing in long, pointed tweezers and a pair with curved ends. They will prove useful for holding and moving small pieces into position.

17 Floristry tape

Floristry tape, or flower tape as it is sometimes known, has a papery mat surface and is used to cover wire stems and add in flowers and leaves to stems and branches. There are many different colours to choose from but the most frequently used in sugar floristry are the natural shades, like light and dark green, white, beige, and brown.

Technique: Cutting floristry tape

Before you begin taping the wire, you may need to cut the floristry tape to a narrower width, usually either ½-width or ¼-width, depending on the item to be taped. You can do this with the aid of a floristry tape shredder or manually: wind the length of tape around two fingers, then slip the tape off your fingers, keeping the loop of tape intact, and proceed to cut along the length as required. Once you have cut the floristry tape ready for use, stretch it to release the glue and make the surface tacky, then wind it around the wire.

Floristry tape can also be used to make some types of leaves, see page 22.

Tip

It is not always advisable to tape down the whole length of each wire if the leaf or flower is to be attached to a spray or leaf formation as it makes the arrangement very thick and bulky. Instead, start underneath the flower or leaf and wind ¼-width (or finer) floristry tape down the wire to the point where the individual stem will be joined to the main stem. Add the next piece into the spray and continue to tape down both wires. Repeat this process until all the leaves and flowers have been added into the spray. The exception to this rule is when you are taping the stems of individual flowers that require a very thick stem (e.g. the calla lily). In this case, you need to tape down the entire stem.

18 Stamens

There are several varieties of stamens available but, in general, small round stamens, seed-headed matt stamens and very fine stamens are most useful when making sugar flowers. They also come in different colours but white is the most versatile as these can easily be coloured with dust or paste food colour.

19 Silk veining tool/friller

Available in either plastic or ceramic material, silk veining tools can be rolled over the surface of petals and leaves to add texture. Among other cake decorating uses, they are an ideal tool for frilling petal edges when a slightly rough effect is required (e.g. poppy petals, see pages 88 to 89).

20 Cotton thread

Fine, cotton thread can be used for making bunches of stamens when a large number is required (e.g. the stamens of a magnolia, see pages 28 to 30, and poppies, see page 86). White thread can be dusted with any food colour to make the correct shade and, as black stamens are fairly common, it is also useful to keep black thread to hand for this purpose.

21 Polystyrene formers

These cup-shaped formers are available in various sizes and are ideal for drying and shaping flowers and petals. Apple trays from the supermarket are also useful for drying flowers, particularly if you have a large number of flowers or petals.

22 Posy picks

For hygiene and safety reasons, floristry wires should never be inserted directly into a cake. Instead, insert the ends of wired flowers and leaves into a posy pick filled with sugarpaste and then position this on the cake top. It is essential to remove all wired decorations from the cake before cutting it and using a posy pick makes this safe and easy to do.

23 Staysoft

An inedible product with similar properties to Plasticine, Staysoft is used by florists as a flower arranging aid. The stems of the flowers can be inserted as many times as necessary until the desired arrangement has been achieved. Sugar florists can use Staysoft for the same purpose or as a means to assemble an arrangement if it is not intended for display on a cake.

PVA glue

Non-toxic PVA glue is used for attaching floristry wire, stamens and floristry tape to sugar flower arrangements. Although this glue is non-toxic, it should not come into direct contact with items that are intended for consumption as it is not an edible or food-grade product.

Food-grade polythene bags

To avoid paste drying out while it is not being used, seal it in a food-grade polythene bag and it will retain its moisture.

Steaming

Steam is used to set dust food colour and create a sheen on finished leaves and petals. Very carefully hold the leaf or petal by the end of the floristry wire and pass the other end through the steam from a boiling kettle. Take care not to hold the sugar in the steam for too long as the petal or leaf will soften and dissolve. Do not touch the leaf or petal until it is completely dry as this can remove the colour.

Glaze cleaner (IPA)

When using confectioners' glaze, it is essential to have glaze cleaner to hand. It effectively removes confectioners' glaze from paintbrushes or surfaces where the glaze has been spilled. It can also be mixed with dust food colours to create quick-drying paint and for diluting confectioners' glaze as mentioned above. NB: glaze cleaner is inedible, so do not consume items which have been coated with a mixture of glaze and glaze cleaner.

Microwave flower press and laminator

I often preserve real flowers and leaves so that I can refer to them, even after they are out of season. The benefit of pressing and laminating the flowers and leaves is that the flower structure will always be preserved (e.g. the number of stamens, shape of the petals,

veining, etc.) and I find it is always better to work from the real thing rather than a picture of it.

Technique: Pressing and laminating flowers and leaves

This can be done using a microwave press (following the manufacturer's instructions) or by pressing the flowers using a traditional method (it is then advisable to laminate the pressed flower for extra longevity). Ensure you open out all the petals to expose the detail in the centre of the flower and make sure the calyx at the back of the flower is unfolded before feeding the flower through the laminator.

Tip

Even after lamination, you will find that the natural colours of some specimens still fade over time so it is a good idea to take some photographs as well.

Edible Materials

Important Note: Although sugar flowers are made, for the most part, from edible products this is only to ensure they are hygienically safe for display on top of celebration cakes. Never consume sugar flowers if they are made with other items that are inedible, e.g. wires, stamens and inedible glazes. If you are making flowers for a cake, always remove them from the cake top before the cake is cut.

Flower paste/Sugar Florist Paste (SFP)

There are many ready-to-use flower pastes on the market, such as Squires Kitchen's Sugar Florist Paste (SFP). Because it is ready-made, the recipe is always consistent and therefore more convenient to use. It also comes in many colours, which is a real time-saver. However, if you would rather make your own flower paste, I have included a recipe below. The ingredient quantities can be adjusted if necessary (e.g. if the paste is too soft, add a little more gum tragacanth, or add cooled, boiled water and white vegetable fat if it is too stiff) and colour can be added before use if required (see paste food colours on page 15). This recipe can also be frozen for later use: simply separate it into smaller amounts and seal in an airtight, food-grade freezer bag.

Tip

Flower paste should always be sealed in a food-grade polythene bag when not in use, otherwise it will dry out.

Flower paste recipe

450g (1lb) icing/confectioners' sugar
15ml (1 level tbsp) gum tragacanth
30ml (2tbsp) cooled, boiled water
14ml (2 heaped tsp) gelatine
20ml (4tsp) white vegetable fat
1 x size one 'Lion Quality' egg – white only, discard the yolk
10ml (2tsp) liquid glucose

Tip

Dip the spoon in cooled, boiled water before you dip it into the liquid glucose, as this will ensure the glucose will slide off the spoon into the mixture more easily.

Important Note: The Food Standards Agency recommends using only pasteurised egg in any food that will not be cooked (or only lightly cooked).

If you decide to use fresh egg white always use eggs bearing the Lion mark, which guarantees that they have been produced to the highest standards of food safety. All Lion Quality eggs come from British hens vaccinated against salmonella, are fully traceable and have a 'best before' date on the shell as a guarantee of freshness.

Eggs can carry bacteria, so always wash your hands before and after handling shell eggs. Cracked or dirty eggs should not be used. Good hygiene should always be practised when preparing any food. For more information and advice, contact the Food Standards Agency or the British Egg Information Service.

Method

1. Place the icing sugar in an ovenproof bowl. Turn on the oven to a low heat and place the bowl into the oven for a few minutes to warm the sugar.

2. Pour the cooled, boiled water into a bowl and sprinkle the gelatine on top. Leave to soak for 10 minutes.

3. Warm the gelatine and water in the microwave or a *bain-marie* to dissolve the gelatine completely. Ensure the mixture does not boil.

4. Add the liquid glucose and white vegetable fat to the gelatine mixture and stir. Set aside to allow the ingredients to dissolve.

5. Gently beat the egg white (do not whisk) then add this, the gum tragacanth and the gelatine mixture to the icing sugar in the warmed bowl. Mix with a warmed beater on a slow speed until all the ingredients have combined. Increase the speed and beat the mixture until it forms a stringy texture (approximately 7 minutes).

6. Remove the mixture from the bowl and knead in some more white vegetable fat if required. Cover the surface of the paste with a layer of white vegetable fat then place it in a food-grade polythene bag and seal in an airtight container. Leave the container in the refrigerator for approximately 8 to 12 hours to allow the paste to mature.

7. The paste will set hard. Break or cut the required amount off the bulk of the paste then knead to soften it and continue until it becomes smooth and pliable. Rub some white vegetable fat onto your fingertips to aid this process.

Technique: Working with flower paste (SFP)

Smear some white vegetable fat onto an area on the surface of the rolling board then roll out the flower paste. To check the paste is at the correct thickness for petals and leaves, place it over a sheet of printed lettering. If you can see the lettering through the paste then it is thin enough to work with.

Lift the paste, turn it over and place onto an area on the surface of the board that is free from white vegetable fat so that the paste will slip and not stick to the board. Cut out the leaf or petal shape you require.

Tip

If the paste dries out whilst you are using it, dip your fingers into cooled, boiled water and knead the water into the paste to soften it. If this makes the paste too sticky, knead in some white vegetable fat.

Paste food colours

Use paste food colours to colour white flower paste or to change the shade of ready-coloured paste. Again, there are many different manufacturers of paste food colours to choose from – I have used the Squires Kitchen Professional range.

Technique: Colouring flower paste

Start by adding a tiny amount of your chosen paste food colour to the flower paste using a cocktail stick. Knead the colour into the paste until it is evenly blended. Repeat this process until you achieve the desired shade then leave the paste for at least half an hour so that the colour can mature.

Tips

- Remember that it is easier to keep adding paste food colour a little at a time to make a darker shade than to try to lighten paste with too much colour added to begin with.

- When strong or dark colours are required, the paste can become quite sticky due to the amount of colour being added. Counteract this problem by adding dust food colour in conjunction with the paste colour.

Dust food colours

Edible dust colours are ideal for enhancing the colour of your sugar flowers or leaves and there is a wonderful range of colours available from a number of manufacturers. Throughout this book, I have used Squires Kitchen's Professional and Pollen Style Dust Food Colours.

Technique: Colouring petals and leaves

Always use dust food colours sparingly. After dipping a dry, flat paintbrush into the dust, rub the bristles on a piece of kitchen towel to remove the excess colour – this will give you more control when you apply the dust to the sugar surface. Once you have achieved the desired colour, you may wish to pass the petal or leaf through the steam from a boiling kettle to set the colour and give a slightly shiny appearance. Allow to dry.

Tips

- Catching the edges of flowers or leaves with a slightly darker colour than the paste is a particularly effective way of enhancing the colour.

- To lighten darker shades of dust food colour, mix them with white (Edelweiss) dust colour. (Cornflour can also be used for the same purpose but the result is not as effective.)

- As more dust colour is brushed onto a flower or leaf, you will notice the paste will eventually stop absorbing the colour. When this happens, carefully pass the flower or leaf over the steam from a boiling kettle. Once it dries, you can apply more dust

colour and the paste will absorb it again. Remember that steam can scald, so always take care when steaming flowers and leaves. Do not steam them for too long otherwise the sugar will dissolve.

Edible glue

Edible glue (or sugar glue) is used to stick pieces of sugar work together. It can be purchased ready-made from your local sugarcraft shop or you can make your own using the following recipe:

Allow 5ml (1tsp) of gum tragacanth to dissolve in 15ml (3tsp) of cooled, boiled water. You can alter the consistency if necessary by adding more water. Store the sugar glue in a small, sterilised pot or jar.

Stronger edible glue for larger repairs can be made by 'letting down' some flower paste with a small amount of edible glue or cooled, boiled water. Adding the water or glue to the paste and working it through well will create a thick, tacky consistency. To ensure the strong edible glue blends into the colour of the piece you are repairing, retain some coloured flower paste for this purpose.

Tip

You will find that, if you use sugar glue sparingly, the pieces will adhere more quickly.

White vegetable fat

Smear a thin film of white vegetable fat onto the rolling board surface to prevent the paste from sticking to it. White vegetable fat can also be kneaded into paste if it is particularly dry and needs softening.

Piping gel

A clear, edible gel that can be used for a number of decorative purposes such as creating dewdrops on leaves and petals. Use a paintbrush to apply it to the sugar.

Food pens

Food pens contain edible ink, which can be used to draw lines or dots onto sugar leaves and flowers. A fine paintbrush and liquid food colours may also be used for this purpose.

Confectioners' glaze

At full-strength, confectioners' glaze creates a strong, permanent varnished effect when applied to a sugar surface. Often, this can be too shiny to resemble the natural look of some petals and leaves so it is advisable to dilute the confectioners' glaze to ½- or ¼-strength with clear alcohol (such as gin or vodka) or glaze cleaner (also known as isopropyl alcohol or IPA).

Technique: Glazing a leaf or petal

The easiest way to glaze a leaf or petal is to transfer the confectioners' glaze into an open-necked jar and dip the pieces into it, holding the end of the floristry wire to which the petal or leaf is attached. Lift the piece out of the glaze but keep it in the jar while you slowly spin the leaf or petal to remove any excess glaze. Hang it to dry on a flower stand or similar. Do not touch the leaf or petal until the glaze has completely dried.

Cornflour/ cornstarch

Cornflour has several uses in flower making: it can be dusted onto the rolling board to prevent the flower paste from sticking; it can be mixed with flower paste to regain the correct consistency if it becomes too tacky (e.g. after adding a lot of paste food colour); and it can also be used to clean paintbrushes after they have been used for dusting – simply dip the bristles into the cornflour then rub them onto kitchen paper to remove the dust food colour.

Making Flowers and Leaves

Each individual flower has its own specific instructions, though there are several techniques that are common in flower making. The terminology and methods are described here, giving an easy reference for many of the flowers in this book.

Flower Making Techniques

Mexican hat

The Mexican hat technique is used to make the basic shape for small flowers like blossoms and calyces for larger flowers.

- Shape the flower paste into a cone then flatten and pinch out the edges of the large end to flatten the paste.

- Stand the cone on a rolling board greased with white vegetable fat and thin the edges of the large end by rolling a CelStick from the middle outwards.

- Place the required cutter over the cone and press out the shape. Lift the cone at the narrow end and turn it flower-side up.

- Use the pointed end of a CelStick to open the centre of the flower/ calyx then widen the indentation with the rounded end.

Cupping

Cupping petals gives them a natural curve, as if they have opened out from the flower centre.

- Place the petal on a foam pad or in the palm of your hand, then soften or shape it by gently rolling a ball tool in the centre, causing the paste to form a cup shape.

Ski stick

The 'ski stick' is used for creating centres of flowers that are particularly large or flat, e.g. the daisy.

- Hold the end of a length of floristry wire with a pair of fine pliers, then wrap the wire around the tip of the pliers to form a loop. Remove the pliers and flatten the loop flush against the length of the wire.

- With the pliers, hold the straight length of wire at the central point of the loop. Bend this point back 90° so that the loop of wire sits horizontally on top of the straight piece of wire, thus forming a 'ski stick' shape.

Making Wired Leaves

Leaves are a very important element of floral displays – they enhance and complement flowers and can even look stunning in an arrangement all on their own, showing off their varying shapes and colours.

There are several methods used for making leaves (which can also be used for petals). When you are new to a craft, I always think it is a good idea to know your options and decide on the method that works best for you.

Whichever method you choose, it is always worth remembering a few basic guidelines:

- Always make spare leaves and petals to allow for breakages before you have completed the project.

- Only use a small amount of flower paste at any one time; you will find it goes a long way and will dry out if it is unsealed and not being used.

- Once the paste has been rolled out, lift it with a palette knife and turn it over onto a non-greased area before cutting out the shape required.

- When using a cutter, ensure you press it onto the paste firmly and jiggle the cutter on the board before pulling the paste away and lifting off the cutter to guarantee a clean cut.

- If you are left with a rough edge once the petal or leaf is dry, gently file it away with a soft emery board (kept for sugarcraft use only).

Instructions for making mahonia, gingko and ivy leaves are given on pages 120 to 121. I have chosen to include these particular leaves as they are all very popular and are useful to add colour and variety to floral sprays.

Method 1: Using a grooved board

To demonstrate this method, I have made a *Cotinus coggygria* (smoke tree) 'Royal Purple' leaf (as featured in Clusters of Carnations, see page 104).

Materials

SK Edible Glue
SK Sugar Florist Paste (SFP): Black, Bordeaux
SK Professional Dust Food Colours: Black, Edelweiss, Leaf Green, Poinsettia
White vegetable fat

Equipment

Ball tool
Floristry tape: brown, white
28-gauge floristry wire: white
Foam pad
SK Great Impressions Camellia Leaf Veiner
Grooved board
Palette knife
Rolling pin
Rose petal cutters: nos. 2RP, 1A, RP1 (FMM)

Method

1. Mix the Bordeaux SFP with a small amount of Black SFP.

2. Lightly grease the grooved board with white vegetable fat. Roll a small amount of SFP over a groove.

3. Cut a 28-gauge floristry wire into three equal lengths. Place one length of wire on the paste over the groove, adding a tiny amount of edible glue to make it tacky if necessary. Fold down the top of the paste over the wire then roll over it with a rolling pin, applying some pressure to ensure the paste sticks to the wire.

4. Use a rose petal cutter to cut out the leaf shape: the pointed end of the shape should be at the base of the leaf. Gently free the paste from the board using a palette knife.

5. Place the leaf into the Camellia Veiner and press down to emboss both sides.

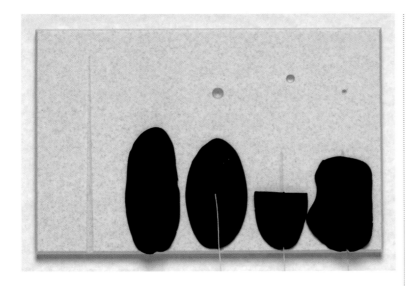

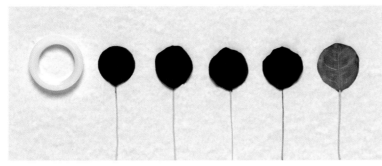

Method 2: Sausage of paste on a wire

To demonstrate this method, I have made a Senecio leaf.

Materials

Clear alcohol
SK Sugar Florist Paste (SFP):
Cream
SK Professional Dust Food
Colours: Edelweiss, Holly/Ivy
White vegetable fat
Cornflour

Equipment

Ball tool
CelStick
Floristry tape: white
28-gauge floristry wire: white
Foam pad
General leaf cutters (TT)
SK Great Impressions Large Tea
Rose Leaf Veiner
Palette knife
Rolling board
Rolling pin
Rose leaf cutters (FMM)

Method

1. Cut the floristry wire into three equal lengths. Roll a small sausage of Cream SFP and gently insert a wire through the middle.

2. Place this onto a board greased with white vegetable fat then roll over it with a

6. Place the leaf on the foam pad and soften the edges using the ball tool (see page 9).

7. Allow the leaf to semi-dry then dust the edges with Poinsettia and the back with a mixture of Leaf Green and Edelweiss Dust Food Colours.

8. Repeat the above steps until you have the number of leaves you need in all three sizes.

9. Starting with one of the smallest leaves, begin to cover the wire with ¼-width white floristry tape. Add in the other leaves one-by-one on alternate sides of the stem, finishing with the largest leaves at the bottom.

10. To add branches to the spray, bend pieces of floristry wire to the required shapes, then cover with brown floristry tape. Once complete, tape the branches onto the main stem.

11. Dust over the length of the stem with Poinsettia mixed with a tiny amount of Black.

Method 3: Thin paste on a wire

To demonstrate this method, I have made a Euonymus (spindle) leaf.

Materials

Clear alcohol
SK Professional Dust Food Colours: Edelweiss, Holly/Ivy, Leaf Green
SK Sugar Florist Paste (SFP): Pale Yellow
White vegetable fat

Equipment

Ball tool
Floristry tape: white
28-gauge floristry wire: white
Foam pad
Food-grade polythene bag
SK Great Impressions Large Tea Rose Leaf Veiner
Palette knife
Rolling board
Rolling pin
Rose leaf cutters (FMM)

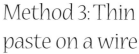

Method

1. Roll a tiny ball of Pale Yellow SFP.

2. Cut a 28-gauge floristry wire into three equal lengths and insert one length into the ball of SFP. Roll the paste down the wire on a foam pad to form a very thin covering at one end. Make several of these.

rolling pin. When the wire is just visible, roll a CelStick outwards from the centre to the edges of the paste on both sides of the wire. Roll over the tip of the paste away from the top of the wire, leaving a ridge down the centre.

3. Cut out the leaf shape then place it onto a foam pad and gently soften and stretch the top edges with a ball tool (see page 9).

4. Vein the leaf using the Great Impressions Tea Rose Leaf Veiner, then use the ball tool to soften the edges once more.

5. Repeat the above steps to make several leaves of varying sizes.

6. Mix some Holly/Ivy and Edelweiss Dust Food Colours together and brush the mixture over the top surface of the leaf, avoiding the edges if possible.

7. Mix some Edelweiss Dust Food Colour with a little clear alcohol to form a white paint. Using a fine brush, paint this around the edges of the leaves. The back of the leaves should remain cream-coloured.

8. Tape the leaves onto one stem, starting with the smallest leaf and adding one at a time on alternate sides of the stem. Increase the size of the leaves as you tape down.

9. To complete the arrangement, make several small stems of leaves and then tape these to the main stem.

Method 4: Wiring a completed leaf

To demonstrate this method, I have made a Euphorbia (spurge) leaf.

Materials

SK Edible Glue
SK Sugar Florist Paste (SFP): Pale Yellow
SK Professional Dust Food Colours: Leaf Green, Marigold
White vegetable fat

Equipment

Ball tool
Floristry tape: white
28-gauge floristry wire: white
Foam pad
SK Great Impressions Large Tea Rose Leaf Veiner
Palette knife
Rolling board
Rolling pin
Rose leaf cutters (OP)

Method

1. Grease a rolling board with white vegetable fat. Roll out some Pale Yellow SFP.

2. Cut out the leaf shape then place this onto a foam pad and use a ball tool to stretch the serrations around the edges.

3. Use the Tea Rose Leaf Veiner to emboss the vein pattern on the leaf surface then repeat step 2 to reshape the edges.

3. Place them into a food-grade polythene bag to prevent the paste from drying out.

4. Roll out the rest of the SFP on a rolling board lightly greased with white vegetable fat. Cut out a leaf shape using the cutter.

5. Place the leaf on a foam pad and use a ball tool to gently elongate the shape.

6. Position the leaf shape on the half of the Rose Veiner that has the raised central vein pattern. Place the wired paste halfway down the centre of the leaf shape then press the other half of the veiner on top of this. When the veiner is removed, the wire will have merged into the back of the leaf.

7. Dust the centre of both sides of the leaf with a mixture of Holly/Ivy and Edelweiss Dust Food Colours.

8. Mix some Holly/Ivy Dust Food Colour with clear alcohol and paint this mixture down the centre of the top surface of the leaf.

9. Repeat these steps to make several leaves of varying sizes.

10. Tape the leaves into groups of twos and threes at the same point using ¼-width white floristry tape. Join these groups together to form one main stem and dust this with Leaf Green Dust Food Colour.

Method 5: Floristry tape leaves

To demonstrate this method, I have made *xerophyllum tenax* (bear grass). This method works especially well for long, thin leaves and very tiny leaves, such as mimosa or daisy.

Materials

SK Confectioners' Glaze
SK Professional Dust Food Colour: Holly/Ivy

Equipment

Floristry tape: dark green
26-gauge floristry wire: dark green
SK Glaze Cleaner (IPA)
Paintbrush (for glue)
PVA glue
Sharp scissors

Method

1. Cut off a length of dark green floristry tape measuring approximately 25cm (10"). Stretch the tape to release the glue.

2. Brush PVA glue over the sticky surface of the tape.

3. Place a 26-gauge floristry wire halfway up along the length of tape then fold the tape over it with the wire down the centre. Press down along the length of the tape and wire then leave this to completely dry.

4. Cut a 28-gauge wire into three. Apply a little edible glue to approximately 1cm (½") of wire at one end, making it only slightly tacky (this is very important as the glue will resist dust colour). Position this on the top surface of the leaf.

5. Lift one half of the paste and fold the leaf in half, laying one side of the paste on top of the other. Very gently press the back surface of the paste near the wire (if you press too hard the two sides of the leaf will stick together) then set aside for approximately two or three minutes. Continue to make more leaves, following the previous steps, while you wait.

6. Open the folded leaf. The wire should now be covered within the ridge created down the centre.

7. Soften the leaf with a ball tool (see page 9) for a more natural look then dust the top surface with Marigold.

8. Brush a tiny amount of Leaf Green Dust Food Colour over the base of some leaves.

9. Tape together several pairs of leaves with ¼-width white floristry tape. Cut out some tiny leaf shapes from white floristry tape, attach these to the top of a pair of leaves and dust with Marigold Dust Food Colour.

10. Tape the pairs of leaves together to make one main stem.

Tip

To give leaves a speckled effect, take a new toothbrush and dip it in your chosen liquid food colour. Use your thumb to brush against the bristles and release the colour onto the leaves. It is advisable to practise the technique on some spare paste first.

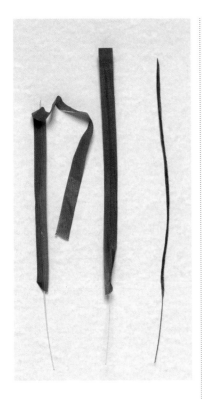

Simple Wiring and Arrangements

Before you start to assemble an arrangement, make sure you have completed all the required flowers and leaves plus a few extra pieces in case of breakages. If you do not use the extra pieces on this occasion, you can always keep them between sheets of kitchen roll or tissue paper and store them in a cardboard box for later use.

4. Using a sharp pair of scissors, cut down one side of the wire to shape the leaf then repeat on the other side. Keep the scissors as close to the wire as possible in order to keep the bear grass leaves very fine.

5. Repeat the above steps to create more leaves in different sizes.

6. Brush the surface of the leaves with Holly/Ivy Dust Food Colour.

7. Dip a paintbrush in the confectioners' glaze and varnish the surface of the leaves. Clean the paintbrush immediately after use with glaze cleaner.

Tips

- Lay a piece of sponge or a soft towel over the area you are about to work on so that, if you do drop anything, it will land on something soft!

- It is better to keep arrangements fairly simple whilst you are learning the techniques to avoid breakages.

Taping a Wire

1. Cut the floristry tape to ½- or ¼-width, depending on the width of stem you would like to make.

2. Stretch the tape to release the glue. Place it under the wire, positioning it just below the flower head or base of the leaf.

3. Holding the wire in one hand, squeeze the tape and the wire between your thumb and forefinger on the other hand and twist it firmly, causing the tape to stick to the wire.

4. Once the tape is attached, continue to tape down the wire for about 1.3cm (½"), keeping the tape as taut as possible, then push the tape up under the base of the flower head or leaf. By starting just below the flower head or leaf to begin with then pushing the tape up the wire, there is less chance of breaking the piece at this stage than if you were to start taping directly beneath the flower or leaf.

5. Holding the tape at an angle against the wire, continue to squeeze and twist the tape with even pressure down the length of the wire. Once the wire is covered, cut or break off any excess tape if necessary.

Tip

Practise this technique on a piece of plain wire before you attempt it on your finished piece.

Posy

A posy is a circular arrangement where the spray is assembled around the central flower or bud. The flowers can be arranged either be a loose posy (various flowers added in the same way as described below) or a formal Victorian posy where circlets of flowers are added around the main central flower in a formalised manner by type or colour.

1. Start by holding the central flower or bud between your thumb and forefinger, just below the base of the flower head. Position a second single flower or bud and tape it to the central flower's stem at the point of your thumb and forefinger.

2. Repeat the step above, adding and taping in one flower, bud or leaf at a time, surrounding the central flower and taping each wire to the main stem at the same point.

3. Gradually increase the length of the stem from the attachment point as you introduce each flower. Each new flower should reach the edge of the previous one to maintain the shape of a gentle arc. Once the posy is completed, tape down the length of the wires, cutting off a few as you go to remove the bulk.

Crescent/ Semi-crescent

The crescent or semi-crescent spray is made in the same way as for the posy but using 'return ends' (a floristry term) to create the curved appearance. The difference between the two is simply that the crescent has a deeper curve than the semi-crescent.

First, make the posy as described above, then make two small, identical sprays with small main stems of equal length. Attach the two small stems either side of the central posy to create the curved ends of the arrangement.

Hogarth Curve or 'S' Shape

This is a long arrangement with a collection of flowers in the centre and trailing ends at the top and bottom, curving in opposite directions to create a gentle 'S' shape. Again, this type of spray can be created using the posy method described above. Once the central posy is complete make two long, curved sprays and attach them to either side of the posy. Alternatively, simply tape together three large flowers as the central, focal point of the arrangement then attach the trailing ends to create a smaller, 'S' shaped spray.

Teardrop/Shower

To create this pear or teardrop shaped spray, tape together some leaves and buds then gradually increase the width up the arrangement. Do this by taping small sprays of leaves and buds, which will make a stem, or an individual unit. Make pairs of different lengths so they can be taped either side of the main stem to create the pear-shape. As the shape forms, larger flowers can be added. A simple way is to use a loose posy technique then make the widening spray and add it to the posy.

'L' Shape

This arrangement has a simple 'L' shape. It is important to remember that the distribution of flowers and foliage is unequal: the height is longer than the base line. These placements of flowers and leaves should be positioned first, either straight or curved, then the central area filled out with shorter stems of flowers and foliage, but maintaining the line shape. Ideally they would be placed into a container or directly into a mound of flower paste and then placed on a cake, therefore eliminating the need for wiring and taping the spray together. (The other wiring techniques described here can also be formed in this way to make arrangements following their guideline shapes.)

Come forth into the
light of things. Let
nature be your teacher.

William Wordsworth

Majestic Magnolia

Magnolia soulangeana has large, chalice-shaped white flowers, tinged with reddish purple around the base. It flowers on bare branches in April and can be quite lovely in an arrangement all on its own or in a spray with other flowers that complement its colours.

Magnolia

(Beauty/Dignity)

Species: Soulangeana

Materials

SK Edible Glue
SK Pollen Style Edible Dusts: Apple Green, Russet
SK Professional Dust Food Colours: Bulrush, Cyclamen, Edelweiss, Holly/Ivy
SK Sugar Florist Paste (SFP): Holly/Ivy, White
Strong edible glue (see page 16)

Equipment

Ball tool
Corn/maize husk
Cutting wheel
Dresden tool
Fine cotton: white
Fine scissors
Floristry tape: brown
22-, 28-, 30-gauge floristry wires: white
SK Great Impressions Tea Rose Veiner (Very Large)
Palette knife
Templates (see page 125)

Method

Flower Centre

1. Roll a ball of White SFP, then shape into an elongated cone measuring approximately 2.5cm (1") long.

2. Push a hooked, 22-gauge floristry wire into the wide end of the cone then reshape the base if necessary.

3. Turn the cone round so that the wired end is at the top. Use fine scissors to make tiny cuts around the base, up to the tip. Gently stroke over the cut edges with your finger to close them slightly and create a more natural effect.

4. Dust the cone with Holly/Ivy and Edelweiss Dust Food Colours. Over-dust with a tiny amount of Cyclamen and set aside to dry.

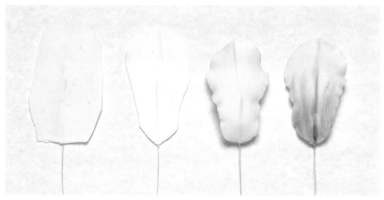

5. Wind the white cotton around two fingers, approximately 30 times. Carefully remove it from your fingers and twist in the middle to create a figure of '8'.

6. Thread a 30-gauge floristry wire through the cotton loop and twist the wire firmly at one end. Use pliers to tighten and twist the wire if necessary.

7. Trim the tips of the cotton into a fan shape, creating lots of individual strands of thread measuring approximately 1.3cm (½") long.

8. Dust the cotton with Cyclamen Dust Food Colour. Apply some edible glue to the ends of the cotton strands. Separate the cotton strands with a pin, then dip the tips into Apple Green Pollen Style Edible Dust. Leave this to dry.

9. Take the cone made earlier and position it so that it sits in the middle of the cotton strands. Use ½-width brown floristry tape to secure both wires and the base of the

cotton together, then adjust the cotton strands so that they are evenly distributed around the cone, creating the stamens of the flower.

Petals

10. Roll out some White SFP and cut around the templates to make nine petals (six large and three small) for each flower. Wire the petals using your chosen method (see pages 18 to 22).

11. Vein the surface of each petal using a corn/maize husk then mark a central vein with the Dresden tool.

12. Take the six large petals, curve the base of each one inwards and pinch the top to shape. Curve the three small petals outwards slightly to form the outer petals. Set aside to semi-firm.

13. Before the petals are completely dry but are firm enough to hold their shape, dust the backs in soft lines

from the base upwards with Cyclamen Dust Food Colour.

Note: The petals need to be assembled while they are semi-dry, so place them in a food-grade polythene bag whilst the others are made.

Leaves

Note: You will only need a few for this spray as this particular plant does not have very many leaves on its branches when the flowers are in full bloom.

14. Roll out the Holly/Ivy SFP and cut out the leaves using the templates.

15. Wire each leaf using your chosen method (see pages 18 to 22) then vein with the Great Impressions Very Large Tea Rose Veiner.

16. Dust with Holly/Ivy Dust Food Colour and set aside to dry.

Buds

17. Roll a sausage of White SFP approximately 5cm (2") long and insert a 22-gauge

floristry wire into the base. Re-form the sausage shape and allow the paste to dry.

18. Roll out some more White SFP and cut out two smaller petals in the same way as before, but do not wire these. Use the corn/maize husk to vein the petals then apply some edible glue to the surface of the wired sausage of paste. Wrap one petal around the sausage then wrap the other around the opposite side so the sausage of paste is barely visible. Cut off the excess paste at the base if necessary.

19. Dust the back of the petals as described for the petals, then roll out some Holly/Ivy SFP and cut out the calyx using the template as a guide.

20. Use a ball tool to soften the edges of the calyx then apply a thin film of edible glue to the surface. Mix Russet Pollen Style Edible Dust with Apple Green then sprinkle this over the calyx and allow to dry.

21. Wrap the calyx around the base of the bud whilst the paste is still pliable. Cover the wire, starting underneath the bud, with ¼-width brown floristry tape. Repeat with a length of full-width tape.

Assembly

22. Use ¼-width brown floristry tape to secure one petal to the wired flower centre, positioning the petal base just underneath the cotton strands. Add another two around the centre, taping all the wires individually to the main stem. Pull the tape firmly so the petals are firm and secure and do not swing around.

23. Position the next set of petals over the gaps between the first three petals so that no two petals are directly on top of each other.

24. Tape down the entire stem with ½-width brown floristry tape then tape over the stem with a final layer of full width tape.

25. For a small spray, take three buds, four open flowers and three leaves. Starting with a bud, tape down the stem with full-width brown floristry tape. Add another bud along the stem.

26. At this point, you may wish to add an additional 22-gauge white wire onto the stem for extra strength. Cut the wire to the required length, place it in position and then tape as normal. Continue to tape down the main stem, then add a small leaf followed by a flower. Continue further down the stem, then add another flower and a leaf. Tape in a bud so that it is slightly higher than the bulk of the spray, giving extra height. Finally, add in the last flower on a longer stem.

27. To texture the branch and stem, scratch the surface with a craft knife. As an extra design feature, add a bunch of light green, slightly curved, 26-gauge floristry wires onto the branch and curve them over the flowers.

For the Cake

Artificial stones
Small spray of magnolias
25cm (10") round cake, covered with white sugarpaste
Round cake drums in the following sizes: 2 x 15cm (6"), stacked, top and sides covered with white sugarpaste; 2 x 20.5cm (8"), stacked, top and sides covered with white sugarpaste; 36cm (14"), top covered with white sugarpaste, covered with ribbon
25.5cm (10") round thin cake board
Royal icing (small amount) or strong sugar glue (see page 16)
Ribbon: white (to cover the drum edge)

Make the most of
the best and the
least of the worst.

Robert Louis Stevenson

Cascading Callas

Named after Italian Botanist, Giovanni Zantedeschi, this beautiful flower can be white, yellow, green, pink, orange or a blackish purple. I have used the white variety to decorate a tiered cake, creating a stylish, modern design.

Calla Lily

(Magnificent Beauty)
Genus: Zantedeschia

Materials

SK Confectioners' Glaze
SK Edible Glue
SK Pollen Style Edible Dust: Pale Yellow
SK Professional Dust Food Colours: Holly/Ivy, Leaf Green
SK Sugar Florist Paste (SFP): Cream, Daffodil, Holly/Ivy, Marigold, White
White vegetable fat

Equipment

Ball tool
Cocktail sticks
Corn/maize husk
Dresden tool
Fine scissors
Floristry tape: light green
20- and 22-gauge floristry wires: white
Foam pad
SK Great Impressions Arum Leaf Veiners: Large
Large arum lily cutter: no. 1123 (FC) or template (see page 125)
Large arum lily leaf cutter: no. 1128 (FC) (optional)
Pliers
Rolling board
Rolling pin
Silk veining tool (HP)
Small, round-headed stamens: white

Method

Centre (or Spadix)

1. Mix equal amounts of Daffodil and Marigold SFP together to achieve the colour for the flower centre. Take a small amount of this paste and shape it into a thin, elongated cone. The centre needs to be approximately ¾ the length of the petal so that the tip sits at the widest point of the petal: to check this, line the arum lily cutter up against the cone.

2. Cut a 22-gauge wire in half (or leave it at full length, if the flower is to hang over a cake edge). Dip the end of the wire into edible glue then insert this into the base of the cone. Reshape the paste if necessary.

3. Turn the spadix upside down and make tiny cuts around the cone about 1.3cm (½") up from the base using a pair of fine scissors.

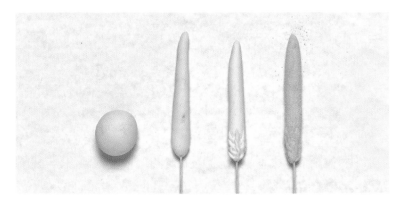

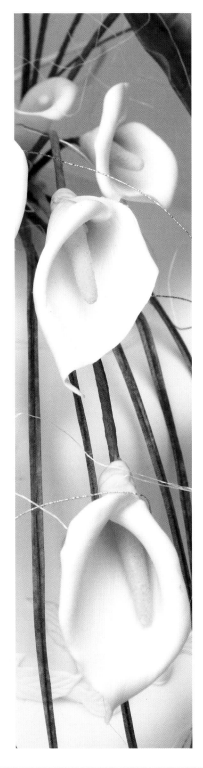

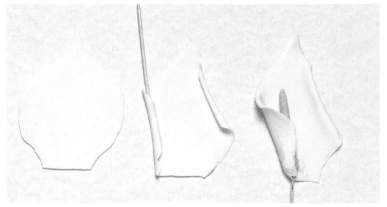

4. Brush edible glue over the flower centre then dip this into Pale Yellow Pollen Dust. Set aside to dry.

Flower

5. Mix together equal quantities of White and Cream SFP. Grease the rolling board with white vegetable fat then roll out the paste, leaving the base area slightly thicker than the top.

6. Cut out the petal shape, positioning the base of the petal cutter over the thicker area of paste. Lift the petal onto a foam pad and use a ball tool to thin the edges. Vein the surface with a corn/maize husk then thin the edges once more.

7. Curl the edge of one side of the petal using a cocktail stick to lift the paste and coax it outwards. Apply edible glue to the base of the petal then place the spadix onto

this. Curl one side of the petal around the spadix then overlap the other side. Bend and curl the top of the petal backwards a little.

8. Round and shape the petal at the base then dust this area and the tip with Leaf Green Dust Food Colour. Hang the flower upside down if necessary until it is semi-dry.

9. Cover the floristry wire with two layers of full-width light green floristry tape.

Leaves

10. Roll out some Holly/Ivy SFP and cut out the leaf shape using the cutter (or use the veiner as a template). Insert a 22- or 20-gauge floristry wire following your preferred method (see pages 18 to 22).

11. Vein the leaf with the Great Impressions veiner then mark the central vein using a Dresden tool. Lightly soften

the edges with a ball tool to create movement (do not frill the leaves).

12. Dust the surface of the leaf with Holly/Ivy Dust Food Colour. Cover the wire with green floristry tape in the same way as for the flower.

13. Carefully pass the leaves over the steam of a boiled kettle to set the colour. Allow to dry then dip into confectioners' glaze and leave to dry.

14. When the leaves are completely dry, use pliers to bend them at a right angle to the wire before assembling them into the spray.

Assembly (Single Bloom)

15. Tape two or three leaves around the base of the stem (or slightly further up if required). If you are using the lilies in a spray, you may wish to add the leaves separately to suit the arrangement.

For the Cake

Arum embosser set (PC)
Bear grass (see pages 22 to 23)
15cm (6") and 25cm (10") cakes, covered with white sugarpaste
35cm (14") cake drum, covered with white sugarpaste, edge covered with ribbon
15cm (6") cake board
6 calla lilies with leaves
Decorative wire: gold
Dowelling rods
Posy pick
Sisal strands (available from florist suppliers)
Strong sugar glue (see page 16)

No matter what
your level of ability,
you have more
potential than you
can ever develop in
a lifetime.

Anonymous

Romantic Rose

There are many methods for making sugar roses – the one shown here is called the 'all-in-one method' using a blossom cutter. It can be used to make roses of any size by varying the size of cutter. Additional instructions are given for making a life-size rose if you wish to present the flower on its own.

Rose

(Red – Love, Yellow – Joy, Pink – Admiration, White – Purity, Orange – Fascination, Lavender – Enchantment, Peach – Modesty)

Genus: Rosa

Materials

SK Confectioners' Glaze
SK Edible Glue
SK Sugar Florist Paste (SFP): Holly/Ivy, Pale Pink, White
SK Professional Dust Food Colours: Cyclamen, Edelweiss, Holly/Ivy, Vine
White vegetable fat

Equipment

Ball tool
Blossom cutter: no. F6 (or FC6 for a life-size, single rose) (OP)
Calyx cutter: R11 (small) or R11E (large for a life-size rose) (OP)
CelStick
Cocktail sticks
Floristry tape: green
24-gauge floristry wire: white
Foam pads (set of 2)
SK Glaze Cleaner (IPA)
SK Great Impressions Large Tea Rose Leaf Veiner
Polystrene flower formers (or apple tray)
Petal cutters: nos. 550, 549 (TT) (only required for a life-size, single rose)
Rolling board
Rolling pin
Rose leaf cutters (FMM)
Silk veining tool (HP)

Method

Centre

1. Make a small hook at the end of a 24-gauge floristry wire. Form a small piece of Pale Pink SFP into a cone shape, making sure it is just smaller than the length and width of a petal on the blossom cutter.

2. Apply edible glue to the hooked end of the floristry wire then insert this into the base of the cone, squeezing the paste around the wire to ensure it is secured. Set this aside to dry. Repeat these steps to make as many centres as you require for your project in advance.

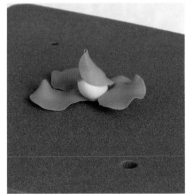

3. Grease a section of the rolling board with white vegetable fat then roll out some Pale Pink SFP quite thinly. Turn the paste over onto a non-greased section of the board and cut out a set of petals with the blossom cutter (use the larger cutter for a life-size rose).

4. Place the petals onto a foam pad and use a ball tool to soften the edges. Brush some edible glue on the centre of the blossom shape then push the wired cone through the middle of the blossom. Place the end of the wire through the hole in the foam pad and then balance the pad on top of a tall glass or container. You now have both of your hands free to work on the rose.

5. Apply edible glue halfway up the length of one petal. Wrap one side around the cone, then wrap the other over the top. The cone should no longer be visible. Miss out the next petal and repeat the process with the third, folding it gently around the first petal and opposite the join.

6. Brush edible glue halfway up the left-hand side of each of the remaining three petals. Stick the first of these to the bud at the same level, leaving the right-hand side free and unstuck. Interlock the next petal so that it is tucked under the previous one and repeat this with the final petal.

7. Gently ease the outer layer of petals downwards, keeping the top of the petals at the same level as the others, and wrap them around the other petals to create a spiral effect.

8. To create an opening rose bud, attach a calyx to the base of the petals at this stage (skip to point 16).

9. Mix equal quantities of White and Pale Pink SFP. Reserve a portion of this mixture then roll out the rest and cut out another blossom shape. Cut away two petals opposite each other then stretch the sides of the remaining three petals with a ball tool. NB: Do not lengthen the petals when you stretch them. Soften the edges of each petal with a ball tool and cup them in the centre (see page 17 for details on cupping).

10. Turn the petals over and use a cocktail stick to curl the edges of each petal from the central point at the top at an angle to the middle point on each side. Place the petals in a flower former and leave them to semi-dry so that they hold their shape.

11. Apply edible glue to the base of the opening bud and feed the prepared petals up the wire. Position the petals so that they stand away from the bud slightly. At this point,

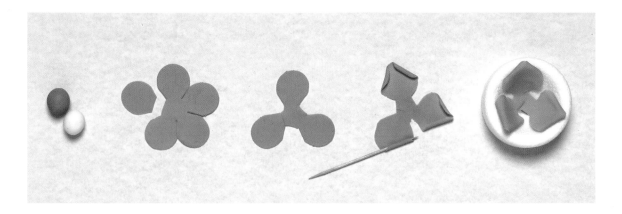

attach a calyx to the base of the flower to form a half-open rose (skip to point 16).

12. Mix the reserved SFP with the same amount of White and roll out this mixture, slightly thicker this time. Cut out another set of the petals using the same blossom cutter. Stretch the petals both lengthways slightly and widthways to make them larger. Cup each petal in the centre with a ball tool then turn the blossom shape over and curl the edges of each petal to the centre point with a cocktail stick, as before. Leave the petals in a former to semi-dry so that they hold their shape.

13. Apply edible glue to the base of the half-open rose then thread the end of the wire into the centre of the petals. Turn the flower upside down and gently arrange the outer layer of petals so that they rest over the edges of the second layer of petals,

overlapping this set of petals but not completely covering them. Gently press the base of the outer petals to secure them in place but ensure they stand away slightly from the previous layer of petals.

14. If you are making a large rose (preferable if it is to stand alone), make two layers of five single, wired petals using the two sizes of petal cutters. Wire the petals using your preferred method (see pages 18 to 22) then vein and curl the edges of the petals, as before. Gently curve each petal at the base and allow to semi-dry. Tape the smaller set of petals around the flower using ½-width dark green floristry tape, then add the larger set around the outside, overlapping the join of first set. Tape each petal individually in place, then allow to dry completely in a flower former.

15. This rose has darker petals in the centre and graduated

lighter petals on the outside. It can be left like this or the contrast can be made more dramatic by dusting the inner petals with Cyclamen Dust Food Colour. Alternatively, you could make all the petals one shade then complete the flower by dusting it in the centre with the darker colour.

Tip

To make a dark red rose, make the flower with full-strength Poinsettia SFP then dust with a mix of Fuchsia and Poinsettia Dust Food Colours. Pass the flower through the steam of a boiled kettle and dust again with the same colours. Brush a tiny touch of Black Dust Food Colour in the centre of the rose.

Calyx

16. Make a Mexican hat shape from Holly/Ivy SFP (see page 17).

17. Place the calyx cutter (use the larger cutter for a life-size rose) over the bump in the paste and cut out the calyx. Turn the calyx over then press the point of a CelStick in the centre and widen the hole with a ball tool.

18. Dust the inside (top) of the calyx with a mixture of Holly/Ivy and Edelweiss Dust Food Colours. Make two or three tiny cuts into the sides of the sepals using fine scissors, then brush edible glue into the centre of the calyx and thread it up the wire onto the back of the rose. Arrange the sepals so that they curl away from the base of the rose slightly.

19. Brush some confectioners' glaze over the calyx to create a natural sheen. When you have finished, immediately clean the paintbrush with glaze cleaner.

Leaves

20. Roll out some Holly/Ivy SFP and cut out the leaf shape. Vein the leaf with the Great Impressions Tea Rose Leaf Veiner then follow your preferred method (see pages 18 to 22) to wire the leaf.

21. Dust the leaf with Holly/Ivy and Vine Dust Food Colours and add touches of Cyclamen on the edges. Steam the leaves and allow to dry.

22. Dip the leaf into ¼-strength confectioners' glaze to create a sheen then allow it to dry again.

23. A stem of rose leaves has one large leaf at the top, two medium leaves below this and then two small leaves. Tape down the leaves for about 2.5cm (1″) with green floristry tape, then tape them close to the central wire opposite each other down the stem.

Tip

If you are short of time a wire can be fixed into the paste by heating the hooked end over a naked flame. Once red hot, push the wire into the paste and it will melt and fuse to the sugar immediately. This method can also be used should a flower fall off its wire. However, ensure you take great care and wear protective gloves if attempting this, as the length of the wire will conduct the heat.

For the Arrangement

2 sets of rose leaves
Single, life-size rose
Small vase

The thing always
happens that you
really believe in; and
the belief in a thing
makes it happen.

Frank Lloyd Wright

South American Beauty

The alstroemeria is celebrated for its beautiful, long-lasting marked flowers. They bloom in many different colours, making them an ideal addition to floral arrangements.

Alstroemeria

(Devotion)
Common name: Peruvian Lily

Materials

SK Edible Glue
SK Professional Liquid Food Colours: Cyclamen, Violet
SK Professional Dust Food Colours: Blackberry, Edelweiss, Fuchsia, Leaf Green, Violet
SK Sugar Florist Paste (SFP): Cream, Holly/Ivy

Equipment

Alstroemeria cutters (FC)
Ball tool
Corn/maize husk
Craft knife
Dresden tool
SK Dusting Brush: no. 10
Floristry tape: light green
24-, 28- and 33-gauge floristry wires: white
Foam pad
SK Great Impressions Large Alstroemeria Veiners
Leaf template (see page 125)
Paintbrush: no. 000
PVA glue
Rolling board
Rolling pin
Small, matte round-headed stamens: white

Method

Stamen

1. Roll a very tiny ball of Cream SFP and attach it to the tip of a stamen. Flatten the paste into more of an oval shape then dust with Blackberry Dust Food Colour mixed with a touch of Edelweiss.

Pistil

2. Cut the heads off of three stamens then stick them together at one end with PVA glue, leaving 1.3cm (½") at the top unstuck.

3. Dust with Violet or Fuchsia Dust Food Colour, depending on the colour you are going to brush on the petals.

4. Cut a 33-gauge floristry wire into three equal lengths. Tape the pistil to a length of wire then stick the stamens around the pistil at a similar height with PVA glue, ensuring that the pistil and stamens are long enough to sit halfway up the length of the petal. Set aside to dry.

Buds

5. Roll a small ball of Cream SFP then mould this into a cone shape.

6. Bend a small hook at the end of a 24-gauge floristry wire. Dip the hook into edible glue then push it into the narrow end of the cone. Reshape the cone, making a point at the tip.

7. Use a craft knife to mark five indentations from the tip downwards. Dust the point with Violet or Fuchsia Dust Food Colour to match the colour of the flower you are making. Brush Leaf Green

Dust Food Colour over the base of the bud.

Petals

8. Roll out some Cream SFP and cut out three inner petals using the narrow cutter. Cut a 28-gauge floristry wire into three equal lengths and insert one into each petal using your preferred method (see pages 18 to 22).

9. Texture the petals in the 7cm Great Impressions Alstroemeria Veiner then place on a foam pad and use a ball tool to soften the edges. Pinch the petal tips and bend the top backwards slightly to give a natural shape. Leave to semi-dry.

10. Mix either Violet or Fuchsia Dust Food Colour with a small amount of Edelweiss then dust both sides of the petal with the mixture. Use the full-strength colour to dust the tips a darker shade. Brush some Leaf Green on the base and draw a soft line up the back of the petal.

11. Draw tiny lines halfway up the middle of the inside of the petal with Cyclamen Liquid Food Colour and a no. 000 paintbrush. Some species only have one petal marked in this way.

12. Repeat these steps to make three more petals but this time using the more rounded cutter and pinching the tips of the petals into more of a point. Curve the top of the petals backwards slightly then leave to semi-dry.

13. Dust in the same way as for the petals made previously, but do not paint the small lines on the inside.

Assembling the Flower

14. Use light green ¼-width floristry tape to secure the spotted, inner petals around the wired pistil and stamen. Add in the more rounded

petals, positioning them over the gaps between the other petals, making sure that no two petals are positioned directly behind each other. Cover the rest of the wire with floristry tape.

Leaves

15. Use the template to cut out the leaves from Holly/Ivy SFP. Insert a 28-gauge floristry wire following your preferred method (see pages 18 to 22). Vein the surface with a corn/maize husk then mark a central vein with a Dresden tool and soften the edges with a ball tool. Dust with Leaf Green Dust Food Colour.

Assembly

16. Tape a group of flower stems together using ½-width floristry tape to form one large branch with all the leaves and flowers positioned towards the top. This is how they grow naturally.

For the Arrangement

Small, glass vase
2 stems of alstroemeria, plus leaves and buds

Life affords no higher
pleasure than that of
surmounting difficulties,
passing from one step
of success to another,
forming new wishes and
seeing them gratified.

Samuel Johnson

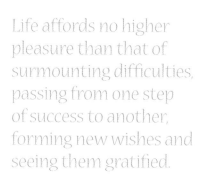

Colourful Combinations

There are around 100 species of Genus Tulipa. They grow in different shapes and sizes and in a vast range of colours, making them a stunning addition to floral arrangements in springtime.

Tulip

(Fame)
Genus: Tulipa

Materials

SK Edible Glue
1 Lion Mark boiled egg (to make the former)
SK Pollen Style Edible Dusts: Pale Yellow, Russet
SK Professional Dust Food Colours: Daffodil, Bulrush, Edelweiss, Holly/Ivy, Leaf Green, Poinsettia
SK Sugar Florist Paste (SFP): Cream, Pale Green, White
White vegetable fat

Equipment

Ball tool
Craft knife
Dresden tool
SK Dusting Brush: no. 10
Fine, pointed scissors
Floristry tape: pale green
18-, 22-, 26-, 28-gauge floristry wire: white
Foam pad
SK Great Impressions Large Parrot Tulip Veiner or corn/maize husk
Palette knife
Rolling board
Rolling pin
Silk veining tool (HP)
Tulip template (see page 125)

Method

Tulip Former

1. Smear the rolling board with white vegetable fat and roll out a thick piece of White SFP. Grease the boiled eggshell with white vegetable fat then mould the SFP around half of it. Allow to one side to semi-dry until the paste holds its shape, then remove the egg and let the SFP dry completely.

Pistil

2. Roll a small ball of Pale Green SFP then mould this into a sausage shape. Insert an 18-gauge floristry wire into one end of the sausage and mould the other end into a more bulbous shape with a pointed tip. Cut off any excess paste to keep the sausage thin. The paste should measure

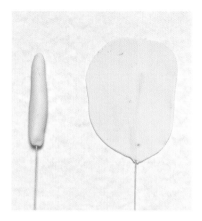

approximately 2cm (¾") in length, so adjust the shape to this size if necessary.

3. Use a craft knife to indent three sections into the tip of the paste. Brush with edible glue then dip it into Pale Yellow Pollen Dust.

Stamens

4. Roll a tiny sausage of Pale Green SFP, measuring approximately 1.3cm (½") long. Insert an unhooked, 28-gauge white floristry wire into the sausage of paste.

5. Roll the tip of the paste to a fine point then dip it into Russet Pollen Dust mixed with a little Bulrush Dust.

6. Repeat these steps to make six stamens per flower. Ensure they are rolled thinly.

Petals

7. Roll out some Cream SFP on a greased rolling board

and cut out the petals using the template. Insert a 26-gauge floristry wire following your preferred method (see Making Leaves on pages 18 to 22). You will need to make six petals per flower.

8. Vein each petal with a cornhusk or Great Impressions Parrot Tulip Veiner. Place on a foam pad and soften the edges with a ball tool. Frill the top of each petal with a silk veining tool.

9. Carefully bend each wired petal to the curve of the former made earlier then place it inside and leave to set off until the paste holds its shape.

10. Dust the edge of the petals with Daffodil Dust Food Colour and the centres with Poinsettia, using the side of a flat paintbrush to create the jagged colouring at the top.

Assembly

11. To assemble the flower, secure the stamens under the pistil using ¼-width pale green floristry tape. Tape three petals individually around the flower centre then tape in the last three, positioning them over the gaps between the first three. (These three petals could be made unwired and glued in place with strong edible glue if preferred.) Continue to tape down the length of the wire then thicken the stem with another layer of full-width floristry tape.

Buds

12. Form a cone shape from Pale Green SFP. Hook the end of a 22-gauge wire and insert it into the base of the cone.

13. Mark three indentations along the length of the cone with a Dresden tool, then use fine scissors to cut into the

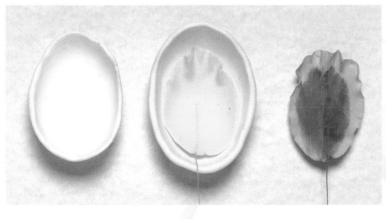

tip of the cone, representing the opening petals. Dust into the open tip with Daffodil Dust Food Colour and brush Leaf Green Dust on the base and sides of the bud.

Opening Buds

14. Model a cone of Cream SFP. Make a hook at the end of a 22-gauge floristry wire, dip this in edible glue and insert it into the base of the cone.

15. Roll out some Cream SFP and cut out three petals using the bud template. Soften the edges with a ball tool and dust with Poinsettia and Daffodil Dust Food Colours in the same way as described for the petals.

16. Wrap the petals around the cone of paste, securing in position with edible glue. Cover the floristry wire with full-width pale green floristry tape.

Leaves

Generally, tulip leaves grow at ground level and the flowers stand in the centre of them, but some species' leaves grown off the stem too.

17. Roll out some Pale Green SFP on a greased rolling board. Cut out the leaves using the template and wire on a 24 gauge wire using your chosen method (see pages 18 to 22).

18. Vein the surface of the leaves with a corn/maize husk then press a central vein in the middle. Dust with a mixture of Holly/Ivy and Edelweiss Dust Food Colours.

The genus Acacia consists of numerous species which are in abundance in Australia (commonly known as wattle), Africa and the Americas. The flowers are small with dense crowds of spiked petals and are a wonderful bright yellow colour in the spring with silvery green leaves.

Mimosa

(Sensitivity)
Genus: Acacia

Materials

SK Edible Glue
SK Pollen Style Edible Dust: Pale Yellow
SK Sugar Florist Paste (SFP): Pale Green,
Pale Yellow

Equipment

Emery board (new)
Fine cotton: yellow
Fine, pointed scissors
Floristry tape: pale green
30- and 33-gauge floristry wires: white
PVA glue

Method

Buds

1. Cut a 33-gauge floristry wire into five equal lengths. Bend a tiny hook into one end of each piece of wire.

2. Roll five tiny balls of Pale Green SFP. Apply edible glue to the hooked end of the wires and push them into the balls of paste. Reshape the balls if necessary.

3. Repeat this process, this time using Pale Yellow SFP and making the balls slightly bigger. Allow these pieces to dry.

4. Brush the yellow balls with edible glue then dip them into Pale Yellow Pollen Dust. Leave to dry once more.

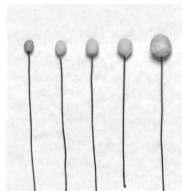

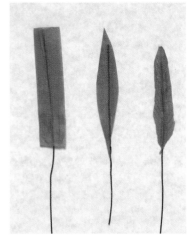

Flowers

5. Wind the fine yellow cotton around two fingers about 50 times. Remove the cotton loop from your fingers and twist it in the middle to make a figure of '8'. Fold this in half to make a smaller loop.

6. Thread a 33-gauge floristry wire through the loop, bend the end of the wire over the cotton and twist it firmly around itself to secure the cotton in place.

7. Cut the cotton opposite the wire to make lots of single strands. Trim these strands down to about 7mm (¼") and arrange them into a fan shape. Hold the strands of cotton together and brush an emery board over the ends to bulk them up.

8. Cover the base of the cotton and the top of the wire with a ¼-width strip of floristry tape.

9. Carefully brush the ends of the cotton with edible glue then dip them into Pale Yellow Pollen Dust. Allow to dry.

Leaves

10. Cut several lengths of pale green floristry tape, measuring approximately 2.5cm (1"), 4cm (1½") and 5cm (2"). You will need to cut six or seven pieces in the various sizes per stem of leaves.

11. Cut a 30-gauge green floristry wire into quarters.

12. Stretch one of the pieces of floristry tape and brush with a layer of PVA glue. Position a piece of wire in the middle of the tape then fold the tape over so that the wire is enclosed in the centre of the tape. Press the tape together firmly. Make about six or seven pieces like this per stem of leaves and allow to dry.

13. Once dry, trim the edges of the tape into a narrow leaf shape. Make tiny diagonal cuts down the leaf from the tip to the base.

14. Use ¼-width floristry tape to secure the leaves together. Start with the smallest at the top then add in a larger pair of leaves further down the stem. Continue taping the leaves in pairs until the stem is the required length.

Assembly

15. Tape the tiny green buds into a clustered group. Tape in the yellow buds, starting with the smallest, and then add the fluffy flowers down the stem.

16. Place a stem of yellow flowers over a stem of leaves and tape them together.

A spring shrub with delicately cupped, blood red flowers that grow off a woody stem. It really complements bold, yellow flowers, adding a touch of warmth and softness to the arrangement.

Japanese Quince

(Temptation)
Species: Chaenomeles speciosa

Materials

SK Edible Glue
SK Professional Dust Food Colours:
Holly/Ivy, Leaf Green, Poinsettia
SK Sugar Florist Paste (SFP): Holly/Ivy,
Poinsettia
White vegetable fat

Equipment

Ball tool
Blossom cutter: F8 (OP)
Craft knife
Floristry tape: brown
28-gauge floristry wire: green
Foam pad
General leaf cutters (TT)
SK Great Impressions Large Briar Rose
Leaf Veiner
PVA glue
Rolling board
Rolling pin
Small calyx cutter (FMM)
Very fine stamens: yellow

Method

Buds

1. Roll a pea-sized piece of Poinsettia SFP into a ball. Make small hook at the end of a piece of floristry wire and push the ball of paste onto the hook. Reshape the paste then mark five small lines, radiating from the centre of the ball of paste, using a craft knife.

2. Roll out some Holly/Ivy SFP on a greased rolling board and cut out a small calyx. Apply edible glue to the centre of the calyx then push the wired bud through the centre and secure the calyx in position at the base of the bud.

Stamens

3. Cut a 28-gauge floristry wire into three equal lengths.

4. Bend five fine stamens in half. Use PVA glue to stick the stamens to a piece of wire then leave this to dry.

5. Cover the base of the stamens and the length of the wire with ¼-width brown floristry tape.

Flower

6. Take a small piece of Poinsettia SFP and make a Mexican hat shape (see page 17), keeping the central bump very small. Cut out a set of petals using the blossom cutter. Place the blossom onto a foam pad and soften the petals with a ball tool.

7. Apply edible glue to the centre of the blossom shape then feed the wired stamens into it, pulling them down into the flower. Allow this to set off, then dust with Poinsettia Dust Food Colour.

8. Cut out a calyx in the same way as for the bud and secure it beneath the flower head.

9. Tape down the wire with ¼-width brown floristry tape.

Leaves

10. Cut out the leaves from Holly/Ivy SFP using the smallest and next-size-up leaf cutters. Vein the leaves using the Great Impressions Large Briar Rose Leaf Veiner.

11. Wire the leaves with 28-gauge green floristry wire following your preferred method (see pages 18 to 22).

Assembly

12. Tape two of the smallest leaves together, positioning one just below the other. Tape in a bud and flower at the same point on the stem. Continue taping down the stem, adding leaves and groups of flowers as you go. Tape smaller stems of flowers and leaves to the main stem if desired.

Sometimes referred to as the Japanese Yellow Rose, Kerria Japonica is a hardy, deciduous shrub which produces a mass of bright yellow, double flowers on long, trailing stems. Accompanied with fine foliage in the springtime, this plant is truly beautiful in full bloom.

Kerria Japonica

Cultivar: Pleniflora

Materials

SK Edible Glue
SK Professional Dust Food Colours: Leaf Green, Marigold
SK Sugar Florist Paste (SFP): Holly/Ivy, Pale Yellow

Equipment

Angled tweezers
Ball tool
Daisy petal cutter set: nos. DY5-DY8 (OP)
Dresden tool
SK Dusting Brush: no. 10
Fine Japanese stamens: white
Fine, pointed scissors
Floristry tape: pale green
22- and 28-gauge floristry wires: green
Foam pad
Food-grade polythene bag
SK Great Impressions Viburnum Leaf Veiners (set of 2)
Rolling board
Rolling pin
Serrated leaf cutter (FC)
Viburnum leaf cutter (FC)

Method

Stamens

1. Take three, very fine Japanese stamens and fold them in half to make six short stamens. Use ¼-width floristry tape to secure the stamens to the end of a 28-gauge green floristry wire which has been cut into three. Ensure you tape approximately 0.7cm (¼") down from the stamen tips, as they should only just peep out from between the petals.

Flowers

2. Thread a tiny ball of Pale Yellow SFP onto the wire up to the base of the stamens.

3. Roll out some Pale Yellow SFP and cut out a set of petals using the smallest daisy cutter. Place on a foam pad, use a Dresden tool to define

the points of each petal and soften the petals with a ball tool. Apply edible glue to the ball of paste at the base of the stamens. Feed the petals up the wire and secure them around the ball of paste. Make and attach another set of petals, forming a small flower.

4. Make four or five small flowers to this stage, then make several more of these so they can be made into larger flowers. Keep them all in a food-grade polythene bag to stop them from drying out too quickly.

5. Using the next-size-up daisy cutter, cut out three sets of petals from Pale Yellow SFP. Place one set of petals onto the foam pad and use a Dresden tool to define the points of each petal, as before. Soften the petals with a ball tool then cup the centres and attach this set of petals beneath the prepared small flower. Repeat the process with the other two sets of petals. This completes the medium-sized flowers. Leave two or three at this stage then continue to make several more for the largest flowers.

6. Cut out two more sets of petals as before, this time using the largest daisy cutter. Attach them to the flower head, below the medium-sized petals.

7. Roll out some Pale Yellow SFP and cut out another set of medium-sized petals. Define the points and soften them with a ball tool as before, then feed them up the wire and attach them to the back of the flower.

8. Dust the petals with Marigold Dust Food Colour and the back of the flower with Leaf Green Dust Food Colour. Pass through the steam from a kettle to set the colour and leave to dry.

Leaves

9. Roll out some Holly/Ivy SFP and cut out the leaves using serrated-edge leaf cutter. Wire the leaves using your preferred method (see pages 18 to 22).

10. Thin the edges with a ball tool then vein the leaves using the larger Great Impressions Viburnum Leaf Veiner.

11. To make smaller leaves, use the same cutter to cut out the leaf shape then use scissors to trim some paste off the base, reducing the size of the leaf but retaining the shape.

12. Dust both sides of the leaves with Leaf Green Dust Food Colour.

Assembly

13. Tape two leaves directly opposite each other on a 22-gauge floristry wire. Attach one of the smallest flowers

just below the leaves then tape down the stem and add another leaf and small flower. Continue to tape down the stem then add a cluster of three leaves and two medium-sized flowers then another three leaves and a single, large flower. Use tweezers to bend the stem into a more zigzag, natural shape.

For the Arrangement

3 tulip flowers, 1 bud, 3 leaves
Glass container
Pebbles (real or sugar)
Piece of fine, twisted wood
Staysoft
1 stem of Japanese quince
5 stems of Kerria japonica
1 stem of mimosa

You could also adapt this design for a celebration cake by inserting the spray into SFP before resting it on the cake top.

If we did all the things
we are capable of doing
we would truly astound
ourselves.

Thomas Edison

Sweet Enchantment

These delicate, butterfly-like flowers are multi-coloured and highly scented, making them the perfect plant to enrich your flowerbeds. Unlike most peas, the seeds are poisonous, so it is a useful flower to make in sugar for celebration cakes.

Sweet Pea

(Blissful Pleasure)

Genus: Lathyrus

Materials

SK Edible Glue
SK Professional Dust Food Colours: Edelweiss, Fuchsia, Holly/Ivy, Leaf Green, Violet
SK Sugar Florist Paste (SFP): Holly/Ivy, Pale Green, White
White vegetable fat

Equipment

Ball tool
Dresden tool
SK Dusting Brush: no. 10
Fine, pointed scissors
Floristry tape: pale green
28-gauge floristry wire: white
General leaf cutter (TT)
Rolling board
Rolling pin
Set of 2 sweet pea cutters: nos. 73, 74 (TT)
Silk veining tool (HP)
Small rose petal cutter (FMM)
Small rose calyx cutter: no. 406 (TT)

Method

Bud

1. Cut a 28-gauge floristry wire into thirds. Bend a tiny hook at the end of each wire.

2. Roll a tiny piece of White SFP into a cone. Flatten the cone slightly, apply some edible glue to the hooked end of the floristry wire and push the cone onto it.

3. Smear a thin film of white vegetable fat onto a section of the rolling board and onto the rolling pin. Thinly roll out a small piece of White SFP on the greased area. Cut out a small petal using the rose petal cutter, then transfer the petal to a foam pad and soften the edges with a ball tool.

4. Brush edible glue onto one side of the petal then fold the petal around the wired cone of paste with the rounded end at the base. Form the petal into a half-moon shape to complete the bud.

Flowers

5. Roll out some White SFP and cut out the winged petal using the cutter. Soften the edges with a ball tool then frill them using the silk veining tool, giving them plenty of natural movement.

6. Brush some edible glue sparingly onto the base and sides of the wired bud. Fold the prepared petal around this, positioning it so that the point of the bud fits through the centre of the winged area with the small point of the petal at the base. Gently squeeze the petal to secure it in place.

7. If you are making a smaller flower that is not yet in full bloom, attach a calyx at this stage (skip to point 10).

8. Cut out a large, single petal from White SFP using the second sweet pea cutter in the set. Insert a 28-gauge floristry wire, following your preferred method (see Making Leaves on pages 18 to 22). Use a ball tool to thin the edges of the petals then frill them in the same way as before. Gently curve the petal backwards and place to one side until it is semi-dry.

9. Use ¼-width pale green floristry tape to attach the wired petal to the wire of the smaller flower. Carefully pull the single petal away from the others to set it in a more natural position. Allow to dry completely.

10. Make a small Mexican hat from Holly/Ivy SFP (see page 17) and cut out the calyx shape. Apply edible glue to the centre then feed it up the wire and secure it to the base of the flower.

11. Dust a few of the flowers with a mixture of Fuchsia and Edelweiss Dust Food Colours and the other flowers with a mixture of Violet and Edelweiss Dust Food Colours. Add more Fuchsia or Violet to the mixture to make a darker shade if desired.

Leaves

12. Roll out some Pale Green SFP and cut out the leaf shape with a general leaf cutter. Insert a 28-gauge floristry wire following your preferred method (see pages 18 to 22).

13. Soften the edges with a ball tool and use a Dresden tool to mark the central vein. Dust the surface with Holly/Ivy and Leaf Green Dust Food Colours.

14. Make the tendrils that grow from the leaf stem by cutting a piece of floristry tape to ¼-width. Roll and twist the tape between your fingers, then curl the strand around a paintbrush handle, remove it and gently pull the tendril to straighten it slightly. Tape three of these pieces together at the base then attach them to the end of a cut 28-gauge floristry wire. Attach the leaves to the base of the tendrils.

Assembling a Spray

15. Cut a length of floristry tape to ⅓-width and use these strips to tape the flowers and buds together. First, take a bud and tape halfway down the wire. Add in two small flowers, again only taping halfway down the wire to prevent the arrangement from looking too bulky.

16. Tape in the full flowers and prepared leaves then begin another stem. Once complete, tape the two sprays together to make one branch then curl the flower stems to create movement.

For the Cake

15cm (6") cake, covered with lilac sugarpaste

25cm (10") drum, covered with lilac sugarpaste, edge covered with ribbon

Posy pick

Several branches of sweet peas

All my life through, the new
sights of Nature made me
rejoice like a child.

Marie Curie

Serenity in Blossom

This is one of many beautiful varieties of ornamental cherry tree grown for their magnificent show of pink blossoms laden on their branches in springtime. This particular species seems to be tolerant of most weathers and can, therefore, flourish at any time of year, but sheds its leaves in winter.

Cherry Blossom

(Spiritual Beauty)
Species: Prunus 'Kanzan'

Materials

SK Edible Glue
SK Professional Dust Food Colours:
Bulrush, Cyclamen, Edelweiss,
Holly/Ivy
SK Sugar Florist Paste (SFP): Holly/Ivy,
Pale Green and Pale Pink

Equipment

Blossom cutter: F10 (OP)
Craft knife
Fine-nosed pliers
Floristry tape: brown, pale green
30-, 33- and 22-gauge floristry wires:
white
SK Great Impressions Rose Leaf
Veiners
Miniature calyx cutter (KB)
Palette knife
Rolling board
Rolling pin
Rose leaf cutters (FMM)
Silk veining tool (OP)
Very fine stamens: white

Method

Buds

1. Cut a 33-gauge wire into four equal lengths and make a tiny hook on the end of each.

2. Roll a tiny ball of Pale Pink SFP. Moisten the hooked end of a wire with edible glue and push it into the ball of paste. Reshape the paste into a ball.

3. Use a craft knife to mark five indentations at the top of the bud. Dust over them with Cyclamen Dust Food Colour.

4. Roll out some Pale Green SFP and cut out the calyx shape. Apply some edible glue to the centre then thread it onto the base of the bud and mould into a natural position.

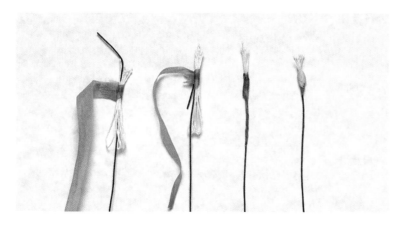

Flowers

5. Bend five fine stamens in half (but do not cut them) to make a group of ten short stamens.

6. Cut a 30-gauge wire into four equal lengths and trim down the green floristry tape to ¼-width.

7. Place a length of wire against the bunch of stamens, positioning the top end of the wire slightly above and parallel to the stamens. Wind the floristry tape 1.3cm (½") below the stamen heads around the stamens and the wire to secure in position. Fold the protruding part of the wire down beside the taped part of the stamens and continue to tape around this part to form a small pad of tape below the stamen heads. The petals will be attached to this later.

8. Trim the ends off the stamens on the diagonal and continue to tape down the length of the floristry wire. This prevents a bulk of tape in one area, creating a smoother stem.

9. Thinly roll out some Pale Pink SFP and use the blossom cutter to cut out the petals. Frill each petal with a silk veining tool then use a ball tool to cup the centres.

10. Apply some edible glue to the base of the stamens, insert the wire through the centre of the petals and feed them up the wire to the base of the stamens. Gently squeeze the SFP around the stamens to hold the blossom in position, forming an opening bud.

11. To make an open flower, make the opening bud as described above. Roll out some more Pale Pink SFP and cut out another blossom shape. Frill the petals, as before, then apply some edible glue in the centre and thread this onto the wire. Squeeze this second set of petals gently around the others to form the open flower.

12. Repeat the above steps to make several opening buds and complete flowers to hang in clusters for one branch of cherry blossom.

13. Dust the flowers a slightly stronger pink with a mixture of Cyclamen and Edelweiss Dust Food Colours.

14. Make the calyces in the same way as for the buds and position these at the base of each flower head.

15. Tape several of the flowers and buds together to form a cluster. Add more of these to form a branch using ¼-width brown floristry tape.

Leaves

Note: There are only a few leaves present when the tree is in full bloom but I like to include them in my arrangements as they add more colour to the overall piece. Make the leaves as you prefer.

16. Roll out some Holly/Ivy SFP then cut out the leaves using the medium and small rose leaf cutters.

17. Wire and vein the leaves following your preferred method (see pages 18 to 22).

Assembly

18. Cover a length of 22-gauge floristry wire with two layers of brown floristry tape, making a thick stem.

19. Tape the branches of flowers and buds, along with some extra bare branches, onto the main stem. Position the wires so that the flowers hang down in clusters.

20. Use a craft knife to cut rough marks into the floristry tape, creating a textured bark effect.

21. Dust some areas with Bulrush Dust Food Colour and other areas of the stem with Holly/Ivy.

For the Cake

15cm (6") cake, covered with white sugarpaste
25cm (10") covered drum covered with white sugarpaste, edge covered with ribbon
Decorative taped wire: beige
Posy pick
Thin satay sticks (or similar)

Anyone who has never made a
mistake has never tried anything new.

Albert Einstein

Country Delight

During the summer months, this beautiful flower paints patches of red on the British landscape. Its green sepals open to reveal four vibrant scarlet petals, crumpled like delicate tissue paper and yet, once fully formed, this flower looks quite majestic as it dances in the summer breeze.

Corn Poppy

(Pleasure)

Species: Papaver rhoeas

Materials

SK Edible Glue
SK Piping Gel
SK Pollen Style Edible Dust: Apple Green
SK Professional Dust Food Colours:
Blackberry, Black, Holly/Ivy, Leaf Green,
Poinsettia, Poppy, Wisteria
SK Sugar Florist Paste (SFP): Pale Green,
Poinsettia

Equipment

Ball tool
Craft knife
SK Dusting Brush: no. 10
Emery board (new)
Fine cotton thread: black
Fine, pointed scissors
Floristry tape: light green
20-, 28- and 33-gauge floristry wires:
white
Leaf template (see page 125) or poppy
leaf cutters (AP)
Paintbrushes
Petal template (see page 125) or poppy
cutter: no. 518 (FC)
Plain-edged cutting wheel
Pliers
Rolling board
Rolling pin
Scriber or glass-headed pin
Silk veining tool (HP)
Tweezers

Method

Stamens

1. Wrap the black cotton around two fingers about 50 times. Carefully slide it off your fingers then twist the loop to make a figure of '8'. Fold this in half to make a smaller loop.

2. Cut a 28-gauge floristry wire into three equal lengths. Thread a piece of wire through the cotton loop then fold it in half over the cotton. Twist the bend of the wire tightly (this will support the ovary) then ensure the cotton is positioned just below this and proceed to entwine the rest of the wire below the cotton, securing it in place. Repeat this step again, positioning the second piece of wire opposite the first.

3. Cut through the middle of the cotton loop, separating the wires and creating two sets of stamens. Trim the ends of the strands of cotton on each to create a fan shape.

4. Rub the tips of the cotton strands over an emery board to bulk them up. Dust the thread with a mixture of Blackberry and Wisteria Dust Food Colours.

5. Brush some edible glue over the tips of the cotton strands then separate them with a scriber or pin. Dip the cotton into Apple Green Pollen Style Edible Dust.

Ovary

6. Roll a small piece of Pale Green SFP into a cone shape. Flatten the top slightly and then use a pair of fine tweezers to pinch about ten ridges into it, radiating from the centre. Allow this to dry a little then dust the ridges with Holly/Ivy Dust Food Colour.

7. Take a set of stamens and tape over the base of the cotton and down the wire with ¼-width light green floristry tape. Open out the cotton strands to expose the tiny twist of wire in the centre. Apply some edible glue to the twist then push the ovary onto it. Set aside to dry completely.

Petals

8. Roll out some Poinsettia SFP and cut out a petal. Insert a 28-gauge wire using your preferred method (see Making Leaves on pages 18 to 22).

9. Soften the edges with a ball tool then texture and frill the petal using a silk veining tool. In this case, the more frilled the petal is, the more natural it will look.

10. Make four petals for each flower then allow them set off before cupping the centres with your fingers. Dust the edge of each petal with a mixture of Poppy and Poinsettia Dust Food Colours. Dust a small triangle shape at the base of both sides of the petal with Black Dust Food Colour.

11. Once the petals are almost dry, start to assemble the flower. The petals will hold their shape as you move them about but they will also be flexible enough to be reshaped slightly once in position if necessary.

12. Position two petals tightly around the stamens then tape these together individually with ¼-width light green floristry tape. Tape the other two petals over the gaps between the first ones so that neither of the outer petals sits directly on top of an inside one. Alternatively,

unwired petals can be glued into this position.

13. If you are making the poppies for an arrangement where they will need to stand upright (as in this project), tape the entire stem of each poppy to another 20-gauge floristry wire for extra support.

Leaves

14. The leaves are made in the same way as described for the petals only this time you will need to use the poppy leaf template or cutter and Pale Green SFP.

15. Insert a 28-gauge floristry wire following your preferred method (see pages 18 to 22). Brush the surface of the leaf with a mixture of Holly/Ivy and Leaf Green Dust Food Colours.

Buds

16. Make a hook in a 20-gauge floristry wire and dip this into

edible glue. Roll a piece of
Pale Green SFP into an egg
shape and insert the glued
wire into the wide end.

17. Use fine scissors to make
tiny cuts from the base
to the tip of the bud to
resemble the fine hairs
found on the real bud. Dust
with Holly/Ivy and Leaf
Green Dust Food Colours
then indent the length of
the bud on each side using
a palette knife.

18. Make some buds with
petals about to unfurl by
inserting a hooked 20-
gauge wire into a small, red
bud. Cut out a single petal
and texture the surface with
a silk veining tool. Brush the
bud with edible glue, wrap
the petal around the bud
and scrunch it up slightly.

19. Dust in the same way as
described for the full flower
and allow to dry. Use a pair
of pliers to bend the wire
beneath the bud into an

arch shape with the bud
hanging down.

20. Roll out some Pale Green
SFP fairly thickly and cut
out two oval shapes (real
poppies have two oval
sepals breaking away from
the stem, revealing the
blossoming flower). Snip
the paste with scissors
to create the textured
surface. Apply edible glue
to the green sepals and
wrap them around the
petal area. Dust with Leaf
Green Dust Food Colour.

Assembly

21. Tape down the stem of
the poppy flower with
¼-width green floristry
tape then add in a bud
or a leaf near the top of
the stem and one further
down (the leaves are
sparse on a poppy). Tape
the buds separately too,
with a single leaf on the
stem.

Commonly found in meadowland, fields, roadsides and hedge banks, the oxeye daisy has an array of white petals with a vibrant yellow centre and is in abundance between June and late July.

Oxeye Daisy

(Marguerite)

Species: Leucanthemum vulgare

Materials

SK Edible Glue

SK Professional Dust Food Colours:
Cyclamen, Holly/Ivy, Leaf Green,
Sunflower

SK Sugar Florist Paste (SFP):
Daffodil, Holly/Ivy, White

Equipment

Ball tool

CelStick

Chrysanthemum cutter: no. 2N
(OP)

Craft knife

Fine, pointed scissors

Fine sieve

Floristry tape: light green

22-, 24-gauge floristry wires: green

Leaf template (see page 125)

Rolling board

Rolling pin

Silk veining tool (HP)

Method

Centre

1. Shape a 22-gauge floristry wire into a ski stick shape, following the instructions on page 17.

2. Roll a small ball of Daffodil SFP, flatten it slightly then secure it to the top of the ski stick with edible glue. Set this aside and allow to dry.

3. Roll another, slightly larger ball of Daffodil SFP and secure this to the previous one. Press a fine sieve against the surface of the paste to create the natural texture of the flower centre. Reshape the base.

4. Use a ball tool to indent the centre slightly then dust with Sunflower Dust Food Colour. Brush a small amount of Leaf Green Dust Food Colour into the centre only.

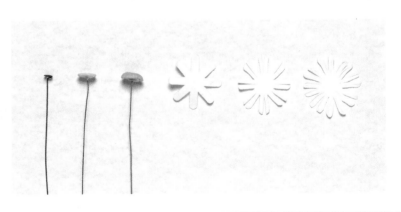

Tip

These petals are particularly fragile so it is advisable to make more flowers than required to allow for breakages.

Petals

5. Roll out some White SFP and cut out a set of petals with the chrysanthemum cutter. Cut each petal in half and roll the silk veining tool over both halves to vein the surface.

6. Repeat step 5 to make another set of petals. Apply edible glue to the centre of one set and secure the other on top. Place into a former to set off. Brush some edible glue onto the petals then push the prepared, wired flower centre through the middle of the two sets of petals and secure in position to complete the flower head.

7. Repeat these steps to make the required number of flowers.

Calyx

8. Roll a small ball of Holly/Ivy SFP and shape it into a cone. Push a CelStick into the thick end of the cone to indent it then use the rounded end of the CelStick to hollow out the cone and to widen and thin the edges.

9. Make tiny cuts into the sepals of the calyx then brush your finger over them to close them up, leaving a scaly surface.

10. Dust the calyx with Holly/Ivy Dust Food Colour then brush a mixture of Cyclamen and Edelweiss Dust Food Colours over the tips.

11. Brush a little edible glue in the centre and feed the calyx up the wire of the flower head, securing it in position beneath the petals.

Bud

12. For an unopened bud, roll a tiny cone of Pale Green SFP. Make a small hook in the end of a 24-gauge floristry wire, insert this into the narrow end of the cone and flatten the top.

13. Use a craft knife to cut tiny slits radiating from the centre of the cone then allow this to dry. Make a tiny calyx as described previously then attach this to the narrow end of the cone.

14. To make an opening bud, cut out a set of petals in the same way as before and secure this around the cone of white paste before the calyx is attached. Use your fingers to close the petals around the cone so that they look like they are unfurling.

Leaves

15. Make the leaves following the floristry tape method (see pages 22 to 23). Cut out the leaf shape using the template then dust the surfaces with Leaf Green Dust Food Colour.

16. Tape the leaves to the flower stem.

Wheat grows in Britain's fields and is as beautiful a plant as it is a useful one, swaying and whispering in the cool summer breeze. It makes a wonderful addition to a wild, natural arrangement of sugar flowers and is relatively simple to recreate.

Wheat

Genus: Triticum

Materials

Cooled, boiled water
SK Edible Glue
SK Sugar Florist Paste (SFP): Cream
SK Professional Paste Food Colour: Marigold

Equipment

Angled tweezers
Craft knife
Dresden tool
Fine, pointed scissors
Floristry tape: beige
22-gauge floristry wire: white
Foam pad
Pastry brush

Method

Wheat

1. Colour some Cream SFP with a tiny amount of SK Marigold Paste Food Colour to make a slightly warmer colour.

2. Cut a 22-gauge floristry wire in half. Insert the end of the wire into a ball of the SFP, then roll the paste into a sausage on the wire, measuring approximately 5cm (2") long. Thin the paste by rolling it on a foam pad. Remove any excess SFP then gently curve the wire and reshape the paste.

3. Roll a tiny ball of the coloured SFP then shape this into an oval, keeping it as small as possible to avoid the finished result looking too bulky.

4. Cut a few bristles from the pastry brush for the wheat's spikelets. Push one bristle into the top of the oval of paste. Reshape the oval if necessary then use a craft knife to mark an indentation down the length of the tiny oval. Make about forty of these pieces per ear of wheat and allow them to dry.

5. Mix some SFP with cooled, boiled water to create a thick, tacky consistency. Thinly spread some of this on to the wired sausage of paste. Stick three spikelets at the tip of the sausage, positioning the bristles so that they stand upright. Continue to attach the other spikelets around and down the sausage of paste, using tweezers to lift and position the tiny pieces.

6. Cover the wire with ½-width beige floristry tape.

Leaves

7. Cut a 5cm (2") piece of beige floristry tape and stretch it out. Cut out the leaf shape and score the surface on a foam pad with a Dresden tool to create a worn, tattered effect. Attach the base of the leaf to the wheat stem by squeezing and twisting the tape onto the stem.

For the Arrangement

Driftwood
8 oxeye daisy stems
SK Piping Gel
8 poppy stems
Staysoft
3 wheat stems

*Every production of
genius must be the
production of enthusiasm.*

Benjamin Disraeli

Wilderness Tamed

Dog roses are a variable species, adding a sprinkling of white to dark pink across hedgerows, scrub, woodland margins and thickets all over the British Isles.

Dog Rose

(Maidenly Beauty)
Species: Rosa canina

Materials

SK Sugar Florist Paste (SFP): Cream, Holly/Ivy, Pale Green
SK Professional Dust Food Colours: Bulrush, Edelweiss, Holly/Ivy, Leaf Green, Rose
SK Pollen Style Edible Dust: Pale Yellow
SK Edible Glue

Equipment

Ball tool
Decorative floristry wire: white
SK Dusting Brush: no. 10
Fine cotton: pale yellow
Fine, pointed scissors
Floristry tape: pale green
26-gauge floristry wire: green
5-petal flower cutters: F5, F6 (OP)
Foam pad
SK Great Impressions Large Briar Rose Leaf Veiner
Pliers
Rolling board
Rolling pin
Rose calyx cutter: R12 (OP)
Rose leaf cutters (FMM)
Scriber or glass-headed pin (sterilised)
Silk veining tool (HP)

Method

Centre

1. Wind the yellow cotton around two fingers about 40 times, keeping a gap between your fingers. Remove the cotton loop and twist in the middle to make a figure of '8'. Fold over to make a smaller loop.

2. Cut a 26-gauge floristry wire into three equal lengths. Feed a piece of wire through the loop, fold the wire over the cotton and move the cotton down slightly to just below the bend in the wire. Twist a small, tight loop where the bend in the wire is then proceed to twist the wire firmly below the cotton so that the cotton is secured in place below the small loop of wire. Repeat this process with another piece of wire positioned opposite the first on the cotton loop.

3. Cut the cotton loop in half, separating the wires and creating two flower centres with stamens. Twist the wire on each one to create a

neat length. Cut the cotton strands to create a semi-circle.

4. Working on one flower centre at a time, tape over the base of the cotton and the length of the wire with ¼-width pale green floristry tape. Open out the cotton strands to reveal the small loop of wire.

5. Roll a tiny ball of Pale Green SFP. Brush a little edible glue onto the small loop of wire and stick the ball of paste onto this, flattening it slightly as you push it into position.

6. Use a scriber or glass-headed pin to prick lots of holes into the green paste. Allow to dry.

7. Brush some edible glue onto the tips of the cotton strands then dip them into Pale Yellow Pollen Dust to create the stamens. Separate these with a scriber or glass-

headed pin, then brush a few stamen tips with Bulrush Dust Food Colour.

Flower

8. Using Cream SFP, make a Mexican hat shape (see page 17). For this flower, keep the raised bump in the centre very small.

9. Use the larger 5-petal flower cutter to cut out the petals. Remove a tiny triangle of paste from the top edge of each petal using the tip of a leaf cutter.

10. Place the flower onto a foam pad and thin the edges and the base of each petal with a ball tool. Gently vein the petals with a silk veining tool and cup the centres. Place in a former to set off.

11. Using a mixture of Rose and Edelweiss Dust Food Colours, dust the edges of the petals on both sides. Brush Leaf Green Dust Food Colour onto the centres.

12. Apply a small amount of edible glue to the centre of the flower and thread the flower centre through the middle of the petals. Secure the prepared stamens in place. Shape the petals to create movement and a more natural look.

Note: These petals can also be cut out using a single rose petal cutter and wired individually.

Buds

13. Roll out some Cream SFP and cut out the petals for the buds using the smaller flower cutter. Remove a tiny triangle of paste from the top edge of each petal, as before.

14. Shape a cone of Cream SFP and insert a hooked and glued 26-gauge floristry wire

into the wide end. Brush the cone with edible glue then push the blossom shape up the wire. Wrap a petal around the cone then miss out the next petal and wrap the following petal around the cone. Continuing to work alternately, wrap the remaining three petals over the first two, securing each one in place with a little edible glue.

15. Dust the petals with Rose Dust Food Colour mixed with a tiny amount of Edelweiss to make a darker shade than the colour used for the open flowers.

Calyx

16. Using Holly/Ivy SFP, make a Mexican hat shape (see page 17).

17. Cut out the calyx with the rose calyx cutter. Using fine, pointed scissors make one or two tiny diagonal snips into the edges of the sepals. Push the calyx up the wire of the bud or flower and secure it in place with edible glue.

18. Dust the calyx with Holly/Ivy Dust Food Colour.

Leaves

19. To make the leaves, follow the instructions for making rose leaves on pages 46 to 47.

Assembly

20. Start by taping a bud and a set of leaves together then add in a flower further down the stem. Continue taping down the stem, adding in the flowers, buds and leaves until you have the desired look for your spray.

21. To complete the spray, tape some decorative white floristry wires onto the stem.

For the Cake

20cm (8") cake, covered with white sugarpaste
38cm (15") board, covered with white sugarpaste; edge covered with ribbon
Posy pick (optional)
White floristry stones (or white sugarpaste/SFP)

Nature never did betray the heart that loved her.

William Wordsworth

Clusters of Carnations

Carnations come in many colours, with different hues symbolising different emotions. They can stand alone in a small spray or can be used to complement other flowers in larger arrangements.

Carnation

(Bond of Affection)
Genus: Dianthus

Materials

Clear alcohol (e.g. gin or vodka)
SK Edible Glue
SK Professional Dust Food Colours:
Cyclamen
SK Sugar Florist Paste (SFP): Holly/Ivy,
Pale Green, White

Equipment

Ball tool
Calyx cutter: CN2 (FMM)
Carnation cutter: C2 (OP)
CelStick
Craft knife
Cutting wheel (PME)
Decorative floristry wires: gold, green
SK Dusting Brush: no. 10
Fine paintbrush
Fine, pointed scissors
26-, 28-gauge floristry wires: white
Foam pad
Pliers
Rolling board
Rolling pin
Silk veining tool (HP)
Small, round-headed stamens: white

Method

Flower

1. Bend a tiny hook in the end of a 26-gauge white floristry wire and thread a small, white stamen through the middle. Bend the stamen in half then squeeze the hook together with pliers to hold the stamen in place.

2. Brush edible glue on the stamen and wire. Roll a tiny ball of White SFP then squash and flatten this over the stamen and wire to hold the stamen together. Allow to dry completely.

3. Roll out some White SFP until it is very thin. Cut out the flower shape using the carnation cutter. Frill the edges of the petals with the silk veining tool.

4. Mix some Cyclamen Dust Food Colour with clear alcohol and paint some fine lines from the centre of the petal to the edge. This will make a variegated flower.

5. Apply edible glue to the centre of the flower and feed it up the wire. Fold the petal in half, sticking the glued surfaces together and creating a fan shape, as shown.

6. Brush edible glue onto the left-hand side of the petals, about 1/3 of the way in from the edge. Fold this section up and back onto itself so that the bottom edge on the left-hand side is now up against one side of the wire. Turn the petals over and repeat this process on the other side. Gently mould and squeeze the base of the petals around the centre to create the rounded base.

7. Cut out another petal then paint and frill the edges as

before. Brush edible glue into the centre and feed the petals up the wire. Gently squeeze the base of the second petal around the first. Leave the flower at this stage if you are making a small carnation or add another petal to make a larger, fuller flower.

8. Once the flower is complete, cut the stamens level with the flower head.

Tip

To make carnations in different colours, use SFP in the required colour then dust a shade darker, e.g. make the petals with Pale Yellow SFP and dust with Daffodil.

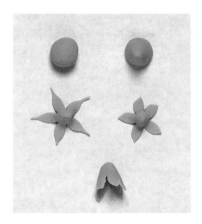

For the Arrangement

7 carnations in your chosen colours (with or without leaves)
Decorative floristry wires: gold, green
Floristry tape: pale green
Small container
2 sprays of cotinus leaves (see pages 18 to 19)
Strong edible glue (see page 16)
SK Sugar Florist Paste (SFP): white

Bud

9. Shape a piece of Pale Green SFP into a cone. Insert a hooked, 26-gauge floristry wire into the base of the cone. Turn the bud over and make five tiny cuts in the base using fine, pointed scissors.

Calyx

10. Make a Mexican hat (see page 17) from Pale Green SFP. Place a small calyx cutter over the central point of the hat shape and cut out the calyx.

11. Lift the calyx off the rolling board and use the point of a CelStick to indent the centre. Widen this indentation with a ball tool.

12. Cut off the pointed tips of the calyx diagonally. Apply edible glue to the centre and feed it up the wire to meet the base of the flower. Round off the base of the calyx and push the sepals upwards.

13. Invert the flower and make five tiny cuts around the base of the calyx using a fine pair of scissors. Gently press these small sections of paste upwards to lie flat against the calyx.

Leaves

Carnation leaves are small and pointed and need to be wired opposite each other in pairs near to the stem. Sprays of carnations can be made without the leaves but I have added them to this arrangement for a more natural look.

14. Add a little White SFP to some Holly/Ivy SFP and blend well to make a slightly paler shade. Roll out the paste, cut out a small, pointed leaf shape using the cutting wheel and insert a 28-gauge floristry wire using your chosen method (see pages 18 to 22). Soften the edges with a ball tool and mark a central vein down the middle.

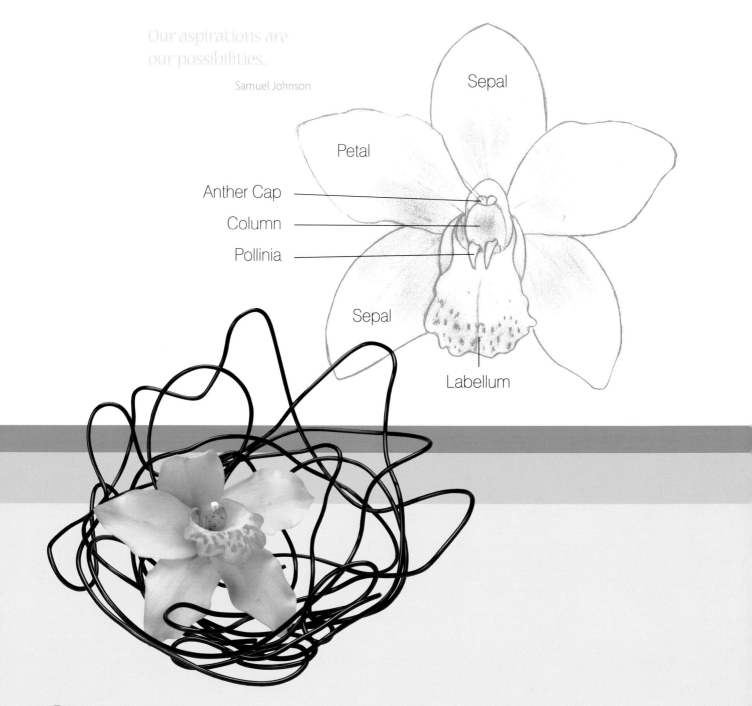

Our aspirations are
our possibilities..

Samuel Johnson

Sepal

Petal

Anther Cap

Column

Pollinia

Sepal

Labellum

Oriental Sunrise

There are numerous species and colours of this orchid, records of which date back hundreds of years. They are popular as pot plants and cut flowers and make excellent focal points in most arrangements, adding an exotic element to the spray.

Cymbidium Orchid

(Refined Beauty)
Family: Orchidaceae

Materials

Clear alcohol (e.g. gin or vodka) or cooled, boiled water
SK Edible Glue
SK Pollen Style Edible Dust: Pale Yellow
SK Professional Dust Food Colours: Cyclamen, Daffodil, Marigold, Nasturtium
SK Sugar Florist Paste (SFP): Cream, Pale Yellow

Equipment

Ball tool
Corn/maize husk
Craft knife
Cymbidium orchid cutters: nos. 16, 17 and 18 (TT)
Dresden tool
Fine paintbrush
Floristry tape: light green
24- and 28-gauge floristry wires: white
Rolling board
Rolling pin
Silk veining tool (HP)

Method

Column

1. Take a pea-sized piece of Pale Yellow SFP and roll into a ball. Shape this into a long cone then press the small end of a ball tool into the wide end of the cone to hollow it out. Use the flat end of a Dresden tool to hollow out the indentation all the way down the length of the cone, paying close attention to the sides to make sure they are thin.

2. Insert a 24-gauge floristry wire into the pointed end of the cone down the back of the shape. Allow to dry.

3. Dust the top of the cone with Nasturtium mixed with a tiny amount of Cyclamen Dust Food Colour then brush Daffodil into the hollowed out area.

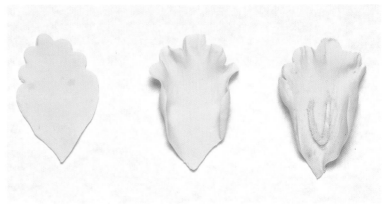

4. Mix Cyclamen Dust Food Colour with clear alcohol or cooled, boiled water and paint tiny dots into the hollowed out area of the cone.

5. Roll a ball of Cream SFP, about the size of the head of a pin, then form this into a tiny oval. Indent it with a craft knife and attach this to the centre of the top of the cone with edible glue.

Labellum (Throat)

6. Roll out some Pale Yellow SFP and cut out the throat of the flower with cutter no. 16. Vein the surface with a corn/maize husk and then thin the edges with a ball tool.

7. Frill the scalloped edges with a silk veining tool then cup the two sides above these edges using a ball tool.

8. Roll a tiny piece of Pale Yellow SFP into a thin sausage measuring approximately 2.5cm (1") long. Bend this in half then secure it at the top of the cupped area. Alternatively, the same effect can be achieved by pinching the pointed end of the labellum with a pair of tweezers, creating two raised ridges in an inverted 'V' shape. Brush the ridges or the sausage of paste with edible glue and then dust with Pale Yellow Pollen Dust.

9. Apply edible glue to the base of the labellum. Fold this around the column made previously then reshape it so that the column is visible and the frilled area is curved down slightly.

10. Dust the base of the labellum with a tiny amount of Cyclamen and Nasturtium Dusts mixed together. Paint small blotches onto the frilled area with Cyclamen Dust Food Colour mixed with clear alcohol. Set aside to allow the paste to dry.

Sepals

11. You will need three wired sepals per flower. Roll out some Pale Yellow SFP and cut out the sepals using the thinner orchid petal cutters. Insert a 28-gauge floristry wire into each sepal using your preferred method (see pages 18 to 22), then vein the wired sepals with the corn/maize husk.

12. Gently curl two sepals backwards and one forwards. Pinch the tips and allow the paste to just set off.

Petals

13. Cut out two petals from Pale Yellow SFP using the wider orchid petal cutter. Insert a 28-gauge floristry wire into each petal using your preferred method (see pages 18 to 22). Vein with the corn/maize husk and gently curl them backwards. Pinch the tips.

14. Dust the surfaces of both the sepals and petals with Marigold Dust Food Colour. Brush the tips and base with Nasturtium mixed with a tiny amount of Cyclamen Dust and allow the petals to set off.

Assembly

15. Assemble the orchid while the petals are still slightly flexible. Use ½-width floristry tape to secure the two petals at the same point, either side of the throat of the flower. Position the inward curved sepal at the top and the other two sepals either side at the base of the flower head. Tape down the stem then allow to dry completely.

16. Once dry, carefully pass the flower through the steam from a boiled kettle to set the colours.

The method used here is for a pulled flower so no cutters are required.

Fantasy Mini Orchid

Materials

Cornflour
SK Edible Glue
SK Professional Liquid Food Colour:
Cyclamen
SK Sugar Florist Paste (SFP): Daffodil,
Soft Peach

Equipment

Ball tool
CelStick
Cocktail stick
Fine, pointed scissors
Floristry tape: green
28-gauge floristry wire: white

Method

Flowers

1. Roll a ball of Soft Peach SFP, approximately the size of a garden pea, then shape this into a cone.

2. Push the CelStick into the broad end of the cone to make an indentation. Close your fingers around the paste and gently turn and twist the cone, thinning it at the open end around the end of the CelStick.

3. Remove the paste and carefully make four cuts into the paste with scissors to define the petals: one large which will be the top of the orchid, a smaller one on either side of this and a medium sized petal at the base.

4. Squeeze all the petal tips individually between your thumb and forefinger to remove the square appearance. Soften the two small petals with a ball tool and pinch the tips again to reshape them.

5. Put some cornflour on your forefinger and place the medium sized petal over it. Gently roll over the petal with a cocktail stick to stretch it, and then pinch the tip. Repeat this with the large petal, making the frilling more pronounced, but do not pinch the tip.

6. Make a small hook in the end of a 28-gauge floristry wire. Hold the flower so that it is facing you with the large, frilled petal at the top then thread the hooked end of the wire into the back of the hole in the flower and push the wire straight down through the paste. The pointed area of paste at the back of the flower is superfluous, so cut straight down the back of the flower, in line with the wire, to remove this paste. Neaten the back of the flower with your fingers.

7. Make a pinhead-sized cone of Soft Peach SFP, flatten and push into the centre towards the back to create a spoon shape. Secure a tiny ball of Daffodil SFP centrally above the thin end of the spoon shape.

8. Mark tiny dots on the petals using Cyclamen Liquid Food Colour.

Buds

9. Make some tiny cone shapes from Soft Peach SFP for the buds and gently push each one onto the end of a 28-gauge wire. Make four indentations to represent the forming petals.

Assembly

10. Tape the buds together first and then add in the flowers to complete the orchid stem.

Bamboo is a woody grass that can grow up to 15 metres tall. There is a vast number of species but all bamboo can be recognised by its familiar stem. These straight stems can add a touch of the exotic to flower displays.

Bamboo

Genus: Arundinaria

Materials

Clear alcohol or cooled, boiled water
SK Edible Glue
SK Professional Dust Food Colours: Bulrush, Chestnut, Edelweiss, Leaf Green, Marigold
SK Sugar Florist Paste (SFP): Cream, Pale Green

Equipment

Ball tool
Corn/maize husk
Cutting wheel
Dresden tool
SK Dusting Brush: no. 10
Fine paintbrush
Floristry tape: beige
18- and 28-gauge floristry wires: white
Foam pad
Leaf templates (see page 125)
Palette knife
Rolling board
Rolling pin

Method

Stem

1. Cut an 18-gauge floristry wire in half. Roll a sausage of Cream SFP and push one piece of wire through the paste.

2. Roll this on a foam pad to thin the paste and work it down the length of the wire, leaving approximately 5cm (2") uncovered at the base for ease of handling.

3. Use a small palette knife to indent a groove around the width of the paste approximately 2.5cm (1") from the top. Repeat this to make another groove below the first, forming a ridge. Repeat this process down the length of the paste.

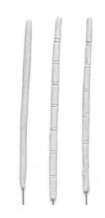

For the Arrangement

2 cymbidium orchids
Bamboo stem
Driftwood
4 fantasy mini orchids with 4
buds
Floristry tape: pale green

4. On the edge of the ridge, make a hole in the paste at the same angle as the wire (this will be where the leaves will be inserted later). Vary the positions of the holes, making some pairs opposite each other at the same level.

5. Create colour washes from Bulrush and Leaf Green Dust Food Colours mixed separately with clear alcohol or cooled, boiled water. Brush these colours over the bamboo stem then set aside to dry.

6. Once dry, dust some areas of the stem with Marigold Dust Food Colour. Mix some Marigold Dust with clear alcohol or cooled, boiled water then use this mixture to paint vertical lines around the stem.

Leaves

7. Roll out some Pale Green SFP and use a cutting wheel to cut out narrow leaves. Using a 28-gauge floristry wire, wire the leaves using your chosen method (see pages 18 to 22).

8. Vein the surface of the leaves with a corn/maize husk then scribe a central vein down the middle with a Dresden tool. Soften the edges with a ball tool.

9. Dust the leaves with Leaf Green Dust Food Colour then allow the paste to set off.

10. Tape the top of the wire of the smallest leaf with ¼-width beige floristry tape then add in the other leaves as you tape down the wire. Make three or four small branches like this.

Assembly

11. Using a fine paintbrush, brush place some edible glue into the holes on the bamboo stem. Trim the wire at the base of a branch of leaves then insert this into the hole. Add the other branches to complete the bamboo.

These are common leaves that you may wish to add to your floral sugar arrangements. You can make each of these leaves by following one of the first four methods described on pages 18 to 22. Although I have included cutters in the equipment lists, the shapes are quite simple to cut out freehand using a cutting wheel if you prefer.

Leaves

Mahonia Leaves

These beautiful leaves are green in the summer and turn a wonderful shades of red, orange and yellow in the autumn, so feel free to adjust the colours to suit the time of year.

Materials

SK Confectioners' Glaze
SK Professional Dust Food Colours:
Marigold, Poinsettia
SK Sugar Florist Paste (SFP): Pale Yellow

Equipment

Ball tool
Dresden tool
Foam pad
Palette knife
Mahonia cutter (FC)
Rolling board
Rolling pin

Method

Follow your chosen method to create the wired leaf then add the veins with the Dresden tool. Dust the leaf surface with Poinsettia and Marigold Dust Food Colours then varnish with confectioners' glaze.

Gingko Leaves

Gingko leaves have a lovely fan-like shape, rather like maidenhair fern. If you'd like some variety in your work, they make an excellent substitute for one of the more commonly used leaves in floral arrangements.

Materials

SK Professional Dust Food Colours: Holly/Ivy, Leaf Green
SK Sugar Florist Paste (SFP): Pale Green

Equipment

Ball tool
Corn/maize husk
Gingko cutters (TT)

Method

Cut out the leaf shape and wire it using your preferred method. Vein the leaf surface by pressing a corn/maize husk over it then soften the edges with a ball tool. Finally, dust the edges of the leaves with Leaf Green Dust Food Colour and brush a tiny amount of Holly/Ivy in the centre.

Ivy

Ivy species are numerous but the most common ones are extremely popular on cakes, especially around Christmastime.

Materials

SK Confectioners' Glaze
SK Professional Dust Food Colours: Cyclamen, Holly/Ivy, Leaf Green
SK Sugar Florist Paste (SFP): Holly/Ivy or Pale Green or Cream

Equipment

Floristry tape: beige or brown
28-gauge floristry wires: green or white
Ivy cutters (JC/FMM)

Method

Make the wired leaf following your chosen method then brush or paint the different green dust colours over the leaf surface. Carefully pass the leaf through the steam from a boiled kettle, allow to dry, then glaze. Tape the leaves onto one stem with beige or brown floristry tape, alternating the leaves down the sides of the stem as you go.

Cake Presentation

If you are displaying sugar flowers on a cake for a special occasion, you will need to think about how the cake is to be presented. Choose a shape and colour scheme to complement the flowers and make sure the cake is the right size for the number of guests. (You can always use an extra cutting cake if necessary.)

Cake size and shape	Quantity of marzipan and/ or sugarpaste
15cm (6") round	450g (1lb)
20.5cm (8") round	800g (1¾lb)
25.5cm (10") round	1.13kg (2½lb)
15cm (6") square	680g (1½lb)
20.5cm (8") square	970g (2lb 2oz)
25.5cm (10") square	1.36kg (3lb)

The quantity of paste required to cover a cake will vary depending on the depth of the cake, so use this chart only as a guide.

How to Cover a Cake

Materials

Buttercream and jam (for a sponge cake) or marzipan, clear alcohol and apricot jam (for a fruitcake)
Cooled, boiled water
Icing sugar
Royal icing (small amount, optional)
Sugarpaste (available in ready-to-use packs from your local sugarcraft shop)

Equipment

Plastic dowel rods
Rolling board
Rolling pin
Smoother
Small, sharp knife
Scriber/glass-headed pin

Preparing the Cake

Rich fruit cake

To prepare a rich fruit cake for the marzipan and sugarpaste coating, trim the top flat. Make a sausage of marzipan and place this around the top edge, sticking it in place with apricot jam. Invert the cake to give a flat, even surface. Use pieces of marzipan to fill in any holes in the cake and the gap around the bottom edge. Ensure the surface is smooth, then brush apricot jam over the surface of the cake. Cover with a layer of marzipan, using the method for the sugarpaste covering below. Allow the marzipan to firm, preferably overnight, then brush with clear alcohol (such as gin or vodka) to dampen the marzipan surface and help the sugarpaste to stick.

Sponge cake

If you are using a sponge cake, cut the top flat and invert it. Fill it with jam and/or buttercream then crumb-coat the surface of the cake with a thin layer of jam or buttercream to seal the cake.

Covering the Cake

1. Knead the sugarpaste until soft and pliable. You may need to dust a little icing sugar onto the work surface if the paste starts to stick to it at this stage.

2. Measure the top and sides of the cake to determine how large the sugarpaste will need to be when rolled out.

3. Dust the work surface with a small amount of icing sugar (do not use too much as it will dry out the paste). Roll out the sugarpaste, rotating the paste frequently to ensure it is not sticking and is an even shape. Do not turn the paste over.

4. The paste needs to be approximately 5mm (¼") thick for a smooth covering. If the paste is too thin the finish will not be as good.

5. Flip the sugarpaste over the rolling pin towards you and lift it up to the prepared cake. (Using the rolling pin to transfer the paste to the cake minimises the risk of marking the paste with your fingers.) Adjust the sugarpaste so the centre of the paste is roughly in the centre of the cake top then gently place it onto the cake top.

6. Smooth the top surface with a smoother, removing any air bubbles from under the paste. Working gradually and evenly around the sides of the cake, ease the paste into place with the palm of your hand, starting at the corners if applicable. Use your other hand to lift the edges of the paste as you work to prevent it from tearing along the top edge.

7. Cut the excess sugarpaste away from the base of the cake using a sharp knife, then gently smooth the surfaces with the palm of your hand. Finally, use a smoother or a pad of sugarpaste covered in cling film to smooth and buff the covering one last time.

Covering the Cake Drum (Board)

There are several ways to cover a cake board, but this is my preferred method.

1. Place the covered cake in the centre of the cake board.

2. Roll a sausage of sugarpaste to the length of the exposed board around the edge of the cake.

3. Cut a straight edge at either end of the sausage then lightly dust the work surface with icing sugar and gently roll out the sausage. Once the sugarpaste is approximately 5mm (¼") thick, cut a straight edge along one side and lightly dust the surface with icing sugar. Roll up the sugarpaste into a coil.

4. Brush a little cooled, boiled water over the exposed cake board and carefully uncoil the sugarpaste around the board, easing the straight edge up to the base of the covered cake.

5. Smooth the surface of the paste with a smoother then trim away the excess paste to neaten the edge. Allow to dry.

Stacking Cakes

1. Place the upper tiers onto thin cake boards of the same size then cover the cakes on the boards as previously described, ensuring the boards cannot be seen. Cover the base tier and the drum as previously described. The cakes should be dowelled and stacked before the sugarpaste dries, so proceed with this straight after the cakes have been covered.

2. Make a template the same size and shape as the cake/s to be stacked. Place the template onto the surface of the lower tier and lightly mark where the next tier is to be positioned, using a scriber or glass-headed pin to indent the sugarpaste surface.

3. Push between four and six plastic dowel rods (depending on the weight of the cake to be supported) within the marked area on the base tier. The denser the cake and the more tiers you use, the more dowels you will need.

4. Use a pencil to mark the point at which each dowel meets the surface of the cake then remove them from the cake.

5. Line the dowels up against each other, ensuring the bases are level, then place a ruler across them, level with the highest point marked on the dowels. Score across this line with a craft knife then trim the dowels to the same height.

6. Reposition the dowels in the cake with the cut end uppermost. Spread a small amount of royal icing between the dowels to show clearly where they are in the cake. This will enable caterers or those cutting the cake to see the dowels easily and remove them safely before the cake is cut.

7. Repeat this process until all the cakes (except the top tier) are dowelled, then carefully stack the cake from the base upwards. Leave the cakes for approximately 24 hours, allowing the paste to set off.

Note: It is advisable to inform the recipient/caterers that they must remove all the dowels (as well as any other inedible items such as ribbon and posy picks) before cutting the cake.

Templates

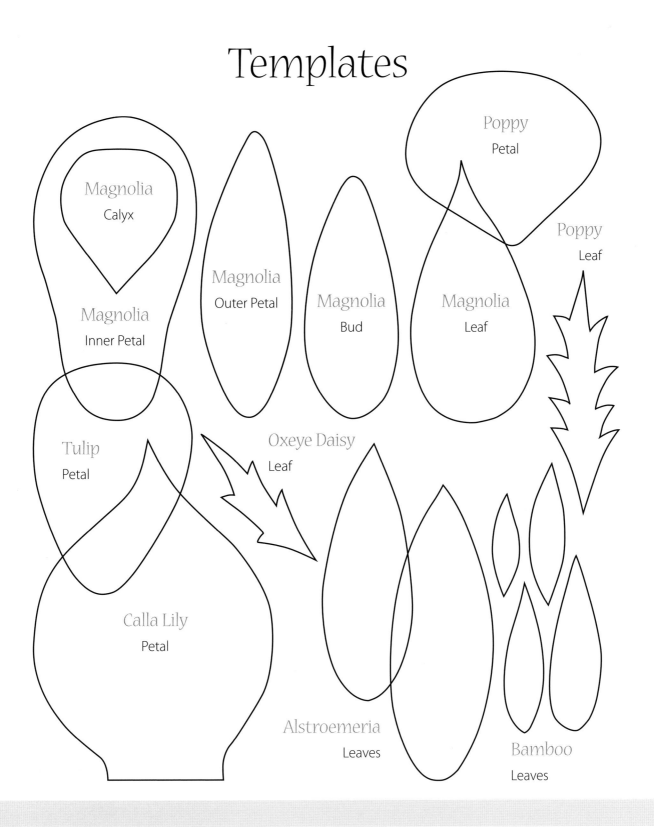

Poppy
Petal

Magnolia
Calyx

Poppy
Leaf

Magnolia
Inner Petal

Magnolia
Outer Petal

Magnolia
Bud

Magnolia
Leaf

Tulip
Petal

Oxeye Daisy
Leaf

Calla Lily
Petal

Alstroemeria
Leaves

Bamboo
Leaves

Suppliers

Shops

Beryl's Cake Decorating and Pastry Supplies

P O Box 1584
N. Springfield
VA22151
USA
Tel: +1 703 256 6951 or +1 800 488 2749
Email: beryls@beryls.com
Website: www.beryls.com

CelCakes & CelCrafts

Springfield House
Gate Helmsley
York
YO41 1NF
UK
Tel: +44 (0)1759 371 447
Email: info@celcrafts.co.uk
Website: www.celcrafts.co.uk

Confectionery Supplies

Unit 11a, b and c
Foley Trading Estate
Hereford
HR1 2SF
UK
Tel: +44 (0)1432 371 451 or +44 (0)29 2037 2161
(mail order)
Email: kclements@btinternet.com
Website: www.confectionerysupplies.co.uk

FMM Sugarcraft

Unit 5
Kings Park Industrial Estate
Primrose Hill
Kings Langley
Hertfordshire
WD4 ST8
UK
Tel: +44 (0)1923 268 699
Email: clements@f-m-m.demon.co.uk
Website: www.fmmsugarcraft.com

Holly Products

6 Kings Court
Welsh Row
Nantwich
Cheshire
CW5 5DY
UK
Tel: +44 (0)1270 625 260
Email: enquiries@hollyproducts.co.uk
Website: www.hollyproducts.co.uk

Orchard Products

51 Hallyburton Road
Hove
East Sussex
BN3 7GP
UK
Tel: 0800 9158 226 or +44 (0)1273 419 418
Email: enquiries@orchardproducts.co.uk
Website: www.orchardproducts.co.uk

Patchwork Cutters

123 Saughall Massie Road
Wirral
Merseyside
CH49 4LA
UK
Tel: +44 (0)151 678 5053
Email: patchworkcutters@btconnect.com
Website: www.patchworkcutters.co.uk

Squires Kitchen Sugarcraft (SK)

Squires House
3 Waverley Lane
Farnham
Surrey
GU9 8BB
UK
Tel: 0845 22 55 67 1/2 (from UK) or
+44 (0)1252 711 749 (from overseas)
Email: info@squires-group.co.uk
Online shop: www.squires-shop.com
Website: www.squires-group.co.uk

Tårtdecor

Bulygatan 14
442 40 KUNGÄLV
Sweden
Tel: +46 303 514 70
Email: info@tartdecor.se
Website: www.tartdecor.se

Tinkertech Two (TT)

See Confectionery Supplies

Distributors

Culpitt Ltd.

Jubilee Industrial Estate
Ashington
Northumberland
NE63 8UQ
UK
Tel: +44 (0)1670 814 545
Email: info@culpitt.com
Website: www.culpitt.com

Guy, Paul & Co. Ltd.

Unit 10, The Business Centre
Corinium Industrial Estate
Raans Road
Amersham
Buckinghamshire, HP6 6FB
UK
Tel: +44 (0)1494 432 121
Email: sales@guypaul.co.uk
Website: www.guypaul.co.uk

Squires Kitchen Sugarcraft (SK)

Website: www.squires-group.co.uk

Manufacturers

AP Cutters (AP)

Treelands
Hillside Road
Bleaden
Weston-super-Mare, B24 0AA
UK
Tel: +44 (0)1934 812 787

Fine Cut Sugarcraft

Workshop 4, Old Stable Block
Holme Pierrepont Hall
Holme Pierrepont
Nottingham, NG12 2LD
UK
Tel: +44 (0)115 933 4349
Email: info@finecutsugarcraft.com
Website: www.finecutsugarcraft.com

JEM Cutters (JC)

P.O. Box 115
Kloof
3640
South Africa
Tel: +27 31 701 1431
Email: jemcutters@jemcutters.co.za
Website: www.jemcutters.com

PME Ltd.

Brember Road
South Harrow
Middlesex, HA2 8UN
UK
Tel: +44 (0)20 8864 0888
Email: enquiry@pmeltd.co.uk
www.pmeltd.co.uk

Squires Kitchen Sugarcraft (SK)

Website: www.squires-group.co.uk

Index

They are able, who
think they are able.

Virgil